1919
Britain's Year of
Revolution

Simon Webb

PEN & SWORD HISTORY

First published in Great Britain in 2016 by
PEN AND SWORD HISTORY
an imprint of
Pen and Sword Books Ltd
47 Church Street
Barnsley
South Yorkshire S70 2AS

ISBN 978 1 47386 286 9

Printed and bound in England
by CPI Group (UK) Ltd, Croydon, CR0 4YY

Typeset in Times New Roman by
CHIC GRAPHICS

Pen & Sword Books Ltd incorporates the imprints of Pen & Sword
Archaeology, Atlas, Aviation, Battleground, Discovery,
Family History, History, Maritime, Military, Naval, Politics, Railways,
Select, Social History, Transport, True Crime. Claymore Press,
Frontline Books, Leo Cooper, Praetorian Press. Remember When,
Seaforth Publishing and Wharncliffe.

For a complete list of Pen and Sword titles please contact
Pen and Sword Books Limited
47 Church Street, Barnsley, South Yorkshire, S70 2AS, England
E-mail: enquiries@pen-and-sword.co.uk
Website: www.pen-and-sword.co.uk

Contents

Chapter 10

Chapter 11

List of Plates

1. The battleship HMS *Valiant*, which was moored off Liverpool in the summer of 1919.
2. A soldier and a tank in the centre of Liverpool during the riots of August 1919.
3. A headline from the *Manchester Guardian* about the disorder in Liverpool.
4. General, later Field Marshal, Sir Henry Wilson, Chief of the Imperial General Staff in 1919.
5. Prime Minister David Lloyd George.
6. Secretary of State for War Winston Churchill.
7. The Red Flag is raised in Glasgow on 31 January 1919.
8. The arrest of David Kirkwood after the 'Battle of George Square' in Glasgow.
9. Glasgow's indoor cattle market being used as a tank depot following the rioting in the city.
10. Troops and police on duty together in Glasgow.
11. Damage to shops near Kinmel Camp after the rioting and gun battle there.
12. The aftermath of the rioting at Kinmel Camp, which cost five lives.
13. Sergeant Thomas Green, the first police officer to be killed in a riot in twentieth-century Britain.
14. A soldier and police officer on guard outside Epsom Police station after the murder of Sergeant Green.
15. A painting by an eyewitness of Luton Town Hall in flames on 19 July 1919. *(By kind permission of Wardown Park Museum)*
16. The burnt-out shell of Luton Town Hall after the riots.
17. Boarded-up shops in Coventry, after the rioting there in the summer of 1919.
18. Police officers on strike in London in 1919.
19. A soldier guards a looted shop in Liverpool.
20. Tanks on the streets of a British city in 1919.

Introduction

A few days before the August Bank Holiday weekend in 1919, a naval officer stationed off the coast of Scotland received an urgent message from London which had him shaking his head in disbelief. The British fleet lay at anchor in Scapa Flow, among the small islands to the north of Scotland. The First World War had ended less than a year earlier and the approaching summer Bank Holiday was the first that the sailors from these ships had enjoyed for six years. There was a more relaxed air than usual, even though the Bank Holiday was not officially being celebrated in the armed forces. The officer who received the message from the Admiralty in London could hardly believe what was expected of the naval forces stationed in this obscure corner of the Orkney Islands. He had received orders to despatch three ships south. One of these was the super-dreadnought battleship HMS *Valiant*. With a displacement of 29,000 tons and armed with 15in guns, the *Valiant* was one of the most fearsome battleships in the world. She may be seen in Illustration 1. What terrible emergency could cause the government to cancel all leave at such short notice and order the *Valiant* into action? The orders were that she was to be ready to put to sea in a matter of hours. In addition to the *Valiant*, two destroyers, HMS *Venomous* and HMS *Whitby*, were also to be ready to sail that day as her escorts.

Obviously, a naval base like Scapa Flow was always on standby, ready at a moment's notice to send warships anywhere in the world that Whitehall should command. It was the destination of the battleship and her escort which was unbelievable. They were to proceed to Liverpool, moor in the Mersey and then land men on the docks and secure them against hostile forces. If necessary, they were then to be prepared to shell an English city to suppress what the government feared was the beginning of a complete breakdown of law and order, perhaps even the opening stages of a revolution. The army had already been deployed in Liverpool, supported by tanks, but had so far been unable to restore order. Illustration 2 shows one of the tanks in the centre of Liverpool.

Today, an account of the events which took place across Britain in

1

1919: BRITAIN'S YEAR OF REVOLUTION

1919 reads like some extravagant fantasy, perhaps an alternate history scenario. Widespread mutinies in the army, tanks brought onto the streets of British cities to crush workers' uprisings, troops imposing martial law on the Bedfordshire town of Luton, a police officer beaten to death in a riot and the government summoning the aid of the Royal Navy to occupy parts of an English port which are under siege from mobs which even the army seems unable to contain. All of this taking place against the background of a British invasion of Russia and fears in the government that a revolution is imminent. To make the point clearer, readers might care to look at Illustration 3, which is a headline from the *Manchester Guardian* of 4 August 1919: 'TROOPS FIRE OVER PILLAGING CROWDS, WARSHIPS DESPATCHED: TANKS ARRIVE'. It is difficult to believe that this is a newspaper report about a British city in peacetime.

It is probably fair to say that very few people are now aware of the perilous state in which Britain found itself in the years following the end of the First World War. Unrest reached such a pitch that Prime Minister Lloyd George told a deputation of strikers quite candidly in the spring of 1919 that they were now in stronger position than the government itself and that if that was what they wanted, then they could take over the running of the country. For a while, it appeared that Britain could be on the verge of transforming itself from a constitutional monarchy and liberal democracy, into a Soviet-style People's Republic.

The precarious situation in which the United Kingdom found itself in 1919 was partly caused, and greatly exacerbated, by the attacks on and invasion of Russia which the British had launched the previous year. Both the ideology and terminology of the Russian Revolution, which had taken place in 1917, spread across Europe, crossing the Channel with ease and being readily absorbed by both the workers and ruling classes in Britain. Expressions such as 'Bolshevism' and 'Soviet' entered common usage and are to be found everywhere in documents from that period; from newspaper editorials to the minutes of Cabinet meetings. Because such terms have, since the collapse of the Soviet Union in 1991, fallen from use, it might be wise to remind readers just what is meant by Bolshevism, and what soviets actually were.

A lingering memory of what was once meant by Bolshevism still crops up from time to time, when an awkward worker shows a tendency to stand on his rights. Such a person might occasionally be described as being 'bolshie', which is of course a truncated form of the word Bolshevism. The Bolsheviks were the revolutionary wing of the Russian Social Democratic Party in the early part of the twentieth century. In 1917, it was the Bolsheviks, led by Lenin, who seized power from the Provisional Government and set up a communist state. In Britain, the term 'Bolshevism' became synonymous at that time with communism and Marxism. Strikers whose demands were regarded as being excessive or unreasonable, were thought to be Bolsheviks and the fear of Bolshevism taking a hold in the country was a very real one for the middle and upper classes.

Another word whose meaning has gradually been forgotten is 'soviet'. Most people remember it now only in connection with the defunct Union of Soviet Socialist Republics or USSR and it is vaguely supposed to be somehow just another, somewhat archaic, word for 'Russian'. The word 'soviet' is no more than the Russian word for 'council' and came, after the abortive 1905 Revolution, to signify workers' committees set up to run factories, towns or army units. After the successful revolution of 1917, a number of other European countries experimented with soviet states, which would be run by councils of workers. All were short-lived and it was thought that some strike leaders in Britain hoped to set up such a system in this country. On 2 February 1920, for instance, a conference of Ministers met in London to discuss the threat of revolution in Britain. A Labour MP in the Coalition government, G. H. Roberts, warned that the industrial action then taking place might be a precursor to a general workers' uprising. He told the meeting, 'There are large groups preparing for Soviet government'.

The idea that a revolution might have been on the cards in this country the year after the First World War ended, probably strikes many readers as being fanciful in the extreme. This is perhaps because of our subconscious preconceptions about the nature of revolution and what such a state of affairs might entail. We tend to imagine troops firing on peaceful protestors, barricades, burning buildings and the storming of palaces and government offices. While it is true that these are indeed the external manifestations of some revolutions, such scenes are by no means an integral part of what constitutes a successful revolution. The transition of power from the state to a new force can take place peacefully, with hardly anybody noticing the process until it has been completed. It is this kind of quiet surrender of government power to a stronger force which almost happened on more than one occasion in Britain during 1919. To see how this kind of bloodless revolution might have happened, it is necessary only to look at the Bolshevik revolution in Russia, which took place in October 1917 and was adopted as a pattern in a number of European countries in the following years.

From February to October 1917, Russia was ruled by a Provisional Government under the leadership of Alexander Kerensky. The loyalty commanded by this government, particularly and crucially in the armed forces, gradually ebbed away until by the autumn the support of the average citizen for the government was lukewarm, to say the least. Many workers and soldiers gave their first allegiance instead to the elected local committees which they themselves had set up, the soviets. When the Bolsheviks decided that the time was ripe, they simply walked into the Winter Palace in Petrograd through an unlocked back door and arrested the members of the Provisional Government who were using the building as their headquarters. Despite all the later propaganda and staged reconstructions of the 'storming' of the Winter Palace, there was no fighting and there were no casualties.

In effect, the taking of the Winter Palace was merely a symbolic act by the new power; the actual revolution had already taken place when ordinary men and women lost faith in the government and refused to support it. The attitude of the army was, as is almost invariably the case during such crises, pivotal. Troops were unwilling to risk their lives for the Provisional Government and instead pledged their first loyalty to their own elected leaders. This was, in effect, precisely what almost happened in Britain in 1919 and the fact that this state of affairs did not, in that particular case, lead to revolution must be regarded more as an accident of history rather than any reflection upon the stability and wisdom of the British state at that time.

Chapter 1

Demobilisation
and The Domino Theory

In the early hours of 5 December 1918, less than a month after the signing of the Armistice which ended the First World War, the British cruiser HMS *Cassandra* struck a mine in the Baltic Sea and swiftly sank. Fortunately, only eleven men were lost, the remainder of the crew being rescued by the destroyers HMS *Westminster* and HMS *Vendetta*, which were both close at hand. All three ships were part of the Royal Navy's 6th Light Cruiser Squadron and they were on active service under the command of Rear-Admiral Edwyn Alexander-Sinclair. The 'War to end War' had finally drawn to a close, with an Armistice being signed only a matter of weeks earlier, yet already, the British armed forces were once again in action. Indeed, it was the considered opinion of the head of the British Army at that time, that despite the defeat of Germany and the collapse of the Austro-Hungarian and Ottoman Empires, the war was not over at all.

One would have thought that four years of the greatest slaughter the world had ever seen might have sated the appetite for war among both statesmen and high-ranking army officers, but even before the guns had fallen silent on the Western Front some members of the British government, aided and abetted by various generals, were planning their next wars. Military action was already being prosecuted against a former ally who posed no threat at all to British interests, the invasion of Russia having begun nine months before the Armistice with Germany with the landing of marines on Russia's Arctic coast. To say that there was no appetite for such a campaign among the ordinary, war-weary soldiers of the British Army, however, would be greatly to understate the case.

When conscription was introduced in Britain, on 2 March 1916, there was no opposition whatever from anybody other than a vanishingly tiny number of malcontents, including some who were devoutly religious and others who were politically left-wing. Out of all the millions of men who were drafted into the army, only 16,500 registered themselves as having conscientious objections to serving in the armed forces. This represented a mere 0.3 per cent of those called up. In other words, 99.7 per cent of those drafted were perfectly happy to join the army and fight against Germany. They did so on the clear understanding that they were being called up to fight until the defeat of Germany. When this object was achieved in November 1918, there was an almost universal expectation among the conscripted men that they would soon be demobilised and sent home. From the Armistice onwards they increasingly regarded themselves, to use an expression current at the time, as 'civilians in khaki'. In fact, both the government and army were, for different reasons, reluctant to allow all the soldiers who had been called up since 1916 to return to civilian life as soon as the war against Germany had ended. There were even plans to extend conscription after the Armistice had been signed.

The army command, from the Chief of the Imperial General Staff General Sir Henry Wilson downwards, had powerful motives for wishing to retain as many men as possible in the armed forces. Some of the reasons were military in nature, others were political. One was neither, but related purely to matters of prestige and power. For much of the twentieth century, the experience of service in the armed forces was so common among British men as to be all but universal. Most people born during the so-called 'Baby Boomer' years from 1946 to 1964 had fathers, uncles and grandfathers who had been soldiers, sailors or airmen. This is in sharp contrast to modern Britain, where it is relatively uncommon to meet former servicemen. It is sometimes forgotten that conscription, in the form of National Service, lingered on in this country until the 1960s. The army was, for over forty years after the end of the First World War, an integral part of the fabric of national life. For perhaps half a century, everybody in Britain had connections one way or another with the armed forces.

In 1918, the army was just getting used to playing this central role in British life, and very pleasant it must have felt to senior officers. During the Victorian Era, soldiers, while they might have been the subject of some sentimental regard by the public, were generally regarded as being an unfortunate necessity. Many public houses would not even allow soldiers on the premises and they were frequently unwelcome at music halls and other places of entertainment. Rudyard Kipling captures perfectly the way that soldiers used to be treated in nineteenth-century Britain in his poem *Tommy*:

> I went into a public-'ouse to get a pint o' beer,
> The publican 'e up an' sez, 'We serve no red-coats here.'

The British soldier may on occasion have been lionised in an abstract sense as the victor of various wars in obscure and out-of-the-way corners of the globe, but in real life he was generally viewed as a troublesome and frequently drunken rogue. Soldiers were certainly not held in the same affectionate esteem that they were during most of the twentieth century.

Having seen the British Army transformed during the First World War in this way, into a national treasure, those running it were reluctant to see it shrink back to its pre-war levels in both numbers and public estimation. Senior officers wished to see a large standing army, well-financed and still furnished with a steady supply of men via the mechanism of conscription. The experience of generals and field marshals such as Douglas Haig and Henry Wilson of being celebrities whose photographs appeared regularly in the newspapers must have been agreeable too, and such men were reluctant to leave the limelight and fade back into obscurity.

Since the early 1960s, it has been the custom in Britain to denigrate the achievements of the senior officers who led the British Army on the battlefields of the First World War. This trend began in 1961, with the publication of Alan Clark's *The Donkeys*, which dismissed the British generals commanding the forces between 1914 and 1918 as 'donkeys', a reference to the supposed description which a German officer gave of the British Army in 1915, that they were, 'Lions led by donkeys'. This revisionist history continued in 1963, with the musical *Oh! What a Lovely War*. More recently, of course, the television comedy *Blackadder Goes Forth* used the same thesis to devastating effect, portraying Field Marshal Sir Douglas Haig as an incompetent and callous fool. This view of men like Haig has become the prevailing orthodoxy over the last fifty years or so, until we cannot imagine anybody regarding the generals of that time as anything other than heartless butchers. The popular perception of the First World War British generals that we have today though, did not emerge until forty years after the end of the war.

During the First World War and for the next few decades, Haig and his fellow generals were regarded with enormous respect and admiration among the general public; not least by the ordinary soldiers who had fought at the Somme, Ypres and Passchendaele. The name 'Douglas' became a popular one in the inter-war years, as old soldiers named their sons in remembrance of the Commander-in-Chief, a man they regarded as their greatest leader. When he died in 1928, an estimated one million people lined the streets for his funeral; such was the esteem in which he was held. He was the people's hero.

Haig and his fellow generals were only human and the adulation which they received during the war must have been quite intoxicating. One could hardly blame them if they wished to prolong their glory, by continuing to preside over a great army and perhaps leading it to even greater glory in other parts of the world. Nor was this desire limited to generals and field marshals like Haig. Even relatively minor officers became public heroes for their military exploits abroad in the years following the end of the First World War in 1918. Men such as Brigadier Reginald Dyer, the Hero of Amritsar, were feted by the British public and their pictures appeared in the newspapers in 1919.

In 1919 Dyer was in command of troops in the Indian city of Amritsar. Fearing that the mood in the Punjabi city could be leading to another rebellion like that of the Sepoys in 1857, he decided to deal ruthlessly with any signs of discontent. When a large group of Indians held an illegal but peaceful meeting, on 13 April 1919, Dyer ordered his troops to open fire on the crowd; killing 379 people. Rudyard Kipling called him, 'the man who saved India' and a public appeal raised the colossal sum of £26,000 (equivalent to about £1,000,000 today), which was presented to Dyer when he returned to England. Dyer became a public figure due to his exploits in the Punjab.

It would be unfair to suggest that the officers in charge of the British Army were only interested in fame and fortune, but there can be no doubt that this was part of the equation. At the same time, they had other, military, reasons for wishing to postpone the end of conscription and the general demobilisation of the armed forces.

To be fair to men like Wilson, who may be seen in Illustration 4, they genuinely believed there to be sound strategic reasons for maintaining a large standing army and delaying the ending of conscription. The recently-ended war had left the United Kingdom with a number of new possessions and there were also serious problems in existing parts of the British Empire, local difficulties which could perhaps be dealt with by the deployment of overwhelming military force. In Ireland, for instance, a rebellion was brewing which it would hardly be possible adequately to tackle other than by the use of armed force. It had already been suggested, when the army was running low on manpower due to the terrible casualty rates on the Western Front, that conscription might be extended to Ireland. This would both have provided the army with another 155,000 men and also perhaps removed many potential insurgents from the country. In the event, although a law had been passed providing for it, conscription had not been adopted there and it was clear that many soldiers would need to be deployed there after the end of the First World War to suppress the outbreak of militant Irish nationalism.

In India, that most prized of Imperial possessions, there was unrest, and there too, nationalism was rearing its head. An urgent need existed, thought the colonial administrators, to increase the strength of the Indian Army. The provinces of Bengal and the Punjab, at opposite ends of the country, were in almost open revolt and strong military action was thought to be necessary to suppress what had the appearance of a popular uprising. Without a greatly strengthened Indian Army, commanders like Dyer would have been hard-pressed to maintain order in the restive province of the Punjab. Neighbouring Afghanistan had been a constant problem for the British for many years; the fear being that the country might act as a conduit for Russian influence or even military involvement, which could jeopardise India itself. That such unease about Afghanistan was justified, was shown when the Third Anglo-Afghan War flared up in May 1919. The Indian Army's role was not of course limited to the Sub-continent itself. Troops from India fought in France during the First World War and later on were also needed in Iraq.

Then again, there were the new possessions of Palestine and Mesopotamia to be considered. One prize which the army had succeeded in snatching even after the Armistice had been signed in November 1918 were the oilfields of Mosul, in modern-day Iraq. Securing the supply of oil from this area was considered by Britain to be a matter of national importance. In addition to defending these oilfields against countries such as Turkey, who were also keen to get hold of the oil, there was also the question of the rebellious Arab tribes who were determined to drive the British from their country. Here too, a large British Army presence was vital to defend the interests of the British Empire. Palestine too was now under British control and could only be held by force of arms.

These were not the only demands being made upon the army in the new world order which slowly took shape after 1918. There were the garrisons at Malta and Gibraltar in the western Mediterranean to be maintained. It was hoped too, to maintain a large and permanent military presence in the Rhineland. Britain was also involved in trying to secure the Dardanelles, the chokepoint linking the Mediterranean with the Black Sea. Finally, of course, there was the little matter of the invasion and occupation of parts of Russia. This entailed a naval presence in both the Baltic Sea and the Arctic Ocean and also a considerable number of troops who would actually be fighting the newly-formed Red Army on land. We shall be looking at this particular campaign in greater detail, both in this and subsequent chapters.

So much for some of the considerations which led to senior officers in the armed forces being reluctant to courtenance a general demobilisation which would reduce the army and navy to their pre-war levels. Some of these same concerns were shared by members of the government, but for Lloyd George's Cabinet there were other powerful reasons for opposing the immediate release of all conscripted men currently serving in the armed forces.

It is customary to describe the war which took place between 1914 and 1918 as being the 'first' world war. There is though a strong case for describing the Napoleonic Wars which raged between 1803 and 1815 and included military action from Moscow to the Middle East, from South Africa to Scandinavia, the Indian Ocean to the Caribbean, as the first genuinely world-wide war. At any one time during this period, one adult British male in six belonged to the armed forces and by the time of the Battle of Waterloo in 1815, hundreds of thousands of men were under arms. The social upheaval caused in Britain by these wars was profound. It was the aftermath of this, the first genuine world war which foreshadowed problems which, thought some members of the government, might be faced in this country in 1919, if hundreds of thousands of servicemen were all discharged simultaneously.

Throughout the early years of the nineteenth century, there were increasing numbers of beggars and vagrants on the city streets and country roads of Britain. Many of these were former soldiers. Patrick Colquhoun, a magistrate and statistician, compiled estimates for the number of unemployed people living rough, and came up in 1806 with a figure of 70,000 for England and Wales, together with another 10,000 travelling performers, circus folk and the like. This was during the early stages of the Napoleonic Wars and the figures rose dramatically, less than a decade later. It is not easy to calculate precise figures, but we may hazard an educated guess from examining what records we do have. In 1810, the Coldbath House of Correction in London, for example, held 265 vagrants. Ten years later, this had risen to 1,287, a five-fold increase. If we then take Colquehoun's estimated number of vagrants and beggars in 1806 and multiply it by five, this might suggest that in the years following the Battle of Waterloo in 1815, there were perhaps 350,000 vagrants, beggars and rough sleepers in England and Wales.

Bearing in mind that only 10 million people were living in England and Wales during the Regency Period and that the population of those two countries has now risen to about 56 million, we can see that the 350,000 or so vagrants would have constituted a significant section of the population. Scaling it up, shows that it would be the equivalent of around two million people today living rough as tramps, beggars, rough sleepers and so on. Many of these, perhaps even the majority, were former soldiers and sailors. By a curious coincidence, the number of soldiers and sailors who were discharged from the armed forces at the end of the Napoleonic Wars in 1815, 350,000, pretty well matches the estimated number of vagrants and tramps who might have been roaming the country in the years following the Battle of Waterloo.

Wandering and unemployed people of this type had, since Elizabethan times, been known as 'Masterless Men' and for centuries they were the folk-devils of respectable citizens, being held responsible for much of the mischief and crime which tended to beset the country in the aftermath of war. The expression 'Masterless Men' signified more than simply men without a master, in the sense that they were unemployed. There was also the suggestion of dangerous and ungovernable men, men who lacked not only a master to oversee them at work, but also any masters in a political or social sense. These people were under nobody's control. It was fear of creating overnight, by means of a general demobilisation, hundreds of thousands of men like this which was very much in the minds of Lloyd George and his Cabinet. Nor were the government the only people who were apprehensive of this supposed danger. The 'Masterless Men' were still a real menace in the minds of many middle and upper class people, as had been the case for over 300 years. Following serious rioting in Wolverhampton in June 1919, after a demobilised soldier had been arrested, the *Manchester Guardian*, forerunner of today's *Guardian*, published an article on 3 June which summed up what many people felt about the ex-servicemen who were now thronging the streets:

> One can hardly imagine trouble on such a scale arising out of an ordinary arrest before the war. Certainly there would not have been such organized defiance of the police. In earlier centuries people shook their heads over the 'masterless men' that the end of a war released on a country. Something of that rare spirit of masterlessness has come in the wake of this war – a readiness to fly to violence and defy authority. Some may put it down to a reaction against discipline and the natural ebullience of men at a 'loose end' after years of restraint. But after three or four years spent in the scientific practice of violence a man does not throw aside the methods he has been so painfully taught by merely changing his clothes.

Returning now to the aftermath of the Napoleonic Wars, the massive influx of rootless and in many cases unemployed army veterans greatly exacerbated the existing political and social tensions in Regency Britain. The rising crime rate, falling wages and increasing unemployment associated with all those hundreds of thousands of discharged servicemen was a contributory factor in the disorder and revolutionary fervour which gripped the country at that time. A few random incidents will indicate the mood of the nation in those years of turmoil.

On 15 November 1816 and then again, two weeks later, huge political meetings were held at Spa Fields in London. The first of these passed off peacefully, but the second, attended by over 10,000 people, degenerated into a riot. A gunsmith's shop was raided for arms and a large body of men set off towards the Tower of London. They were intercepted by troops. A few months later, on 28 January 1817, the Prince Regent's coach was attacked on the way back from Parliament. The government reacted by suspending Habeas Corpus. A few weeks later, thousands of textile workers in Manchester, the so-called 'Blanketeers', began what was supposed to be a march to London; the aim of which was to petition the Prince Regent over the heads of Parliament. Thousands of men set off, with the avowed intent of protesting about the starvation they faced due to the adverse economic situation. Troops surrounded them after a short distance and cavalry dispersed the demonstrators by using their sabres against them. A number of people were injured and one onlooker was shot dead.

Unrest continued, including the notorious 'Peterloo' massacre at St. Peter's Fields in Manchester on 18 August 1819, when cavalry attacked a peaceful demonstration, killing eleven people. In 1820 came the Cato Street Conspiracy, in which a group of revolutionaries planned to assassinate the Prime Minister Lord Liverpool and his entire Cabinet and then to seize the capital. Five of those found guilty of this plot were executed on 1 May 1820. So concerned was the government about the possible ramifications of this projected coup, that on the day that the men were hanged, troops were stationed near the prison and artillery was positioned at key points across London.

This then was the previous experience in Britain of a world war ending and hundreds of thousands of soldiers and sailors being simultaneously demobilised that Lloyd George and his government had in mind when they made plans for the disposition of the armed forces after the Armistice in 1918. Quite apart from the military considerations urged upon them by various senior officers, they wished at all costs to avoid a repetition of the disorder and sedition which had plagued the country in the years which followed the end of the Napoleonic Wars. It was plain that unemployment might rise and keeping a large number of men under arms would ameliorate this. There were two more factors at play when thinking about a general demobilisation of the sort that everybody other than the government and army felt to be both necessary and desirable.

Having hundreds of thousands of discontented men wandering about the country without work and sometimes without even somewhere to live is of course not a prospect to be relished under any circumstances. When the men in question are former soldiers who have been serving overseas for years, this adds an entirely new dimension to the problem. These are men for whom danger has been a way of life and they are often bolder and more likely to take rash actions than the average citizen. Having lived in the danger of death for long periods of time changes people and alters the way that they think. As the *Manchester Guardian* put it so neatly, the last three or four years of these men's lives had been 'spent in the scientific practice of violence'.

Add to this the fact that here were men who had lived under the most ferocious discipline for years, including the threat of the death penalty for such relatively minor offences as sleeping on guard duty, and were now able to do pretty much as they pleased. Then again, men who have been serving overseas have seen different ways of doing things, learned about strange new ideas. They know that the traditional way of life in Britain is not the only possible way of living and ordering society. One final point is that soldiers have been trained to kill their enemies without hesitation and taught to use all manner of deadly weapons. Little wonder that the British Cabinet in 1918 wished to avoid large numbers of such men milling around the streets of industrial cities where they might have no jobs to go to and nothing to do but stand on street corners, discussing their grievances with other like-minded souls!

The revolutionary atmosphere which precipitated many of the confrontations between the government and working people in Regency Britain had been stimulated, encouraged and, some said, even caused by the example of a European country which had recently overthrown and executed its monarch. In the late eighteenth and early nineteenth century, discontented workers and former soldiers could look to France as a model for what might be achieved if enough of them banded together and acted with determination. So pernicious had been the influence of the ideas of Revolutionary France that many among the ruling class of Britain believed that without this example to follow, much of the sedition in this country would simply not have existed. In 1918, there were those in Lloyd George's government, Winston Churchill for example, who saw precisely the same thing happening; only this time, they believed that it might be possible to do something about it. Lloyd George and Winston Churchill are shown in Illustrations 5 and 6.

In the early spring of 1917, the Russian people had deposed their monarch, Tsar Nicholas II, and set up a Provisional Government led by Alexander Kerensky to rule their country. Eight months later, communists overthrew the Provisional Government and seized power in a *coup d'état*. The Tsar and his family were subsequently murdered. This was all very alarming to the allied governments of Britain, France and the United States, because apart from anything else, it mean that after making peace with a fatally weakened Russia, the Germans were now free to direct the whole of their military efforts against the Western Front. From the British and American perspective in particular though, there was an even greater danger than just seeing more German soldiers arriving to reinforce their lines on the Western Front. There was also the direct threat, as it was supposed to be, that communism might spread westwards from Russia and infect first Europe and then, ultimately, the world; including the United States of America.

During the period after the end of the Second World War which became known as the Cold War, a concept called the 'Domino Theory' became popular. This was the idea that once one country had, as it was then said, 'fallen' to communism, then neighbouring countries would also be vulnerable to communist infiltration and eventually at risk of being taken over by communists themselves. At first, this theory was applied only to South-East Asia, with it being suggested that countries such as North Korea and North Vietnam might affect other countries like Laos, Cambodia, Burma, Thailand and even, in the end, Japan and Indonesia. Like a line of dominoes, as one toppled over, others would follow. Later, the Domino Theory was thought to shed light on geo-political developments in Africa and the Middle East.

As 1918 drew to a close, there were those in the British government who saw a similar situation as that which a later generation would believe to exist at the height of the Cold War. In 1917, Russia had become the first country in the world to be ruled by leaders who were followers of Karl Marx's political and economic theories. It seemed as though communism was now indeed spreading to other nations. It is sometimes forgotten that the end of the First World War came only when the Kaiser had been overthrown by mutinies in the German armed forces and workers' uprisings. In the aftermath of the German Revolution, a number of Soviet Republics were established in Europe. Some were in Germany, others in Hungary and elsewhere. All were influenced and inspired by the example of Russia.

Almost a year before the end of the First World War, communists seized control of the Latvian city of Riga and administered it for five months, until May 1918. In Finland, a civil war was fought, with one side hoping to see Finland becoming the first Soviet Republic outside Russia itself. These events were sufficiently far from Britain to be viewed, at first, as of no great significance for those living in the more prosperous and settled countries in the west of the continent.

The first place in Western Europe to see the overthrow of a monarch and subsequent setting up a republic was the German state of Bavaria, which had been ruled for over 700 years by the Wittelsbach dynasty. On 7 November 1918, King Ludwig III of Bavaria was deposed. The republic which was set up after the King's abdication was replaced after a short time by a Soviet Republic, which ended in bloodshed in Munich on 3 May 1919. Another Soviet Republic was set up in the German city of Bremen at about the same time. On 10 November, yet another Soviet Republic was declared; this time in Strasbourg. The Alsace Soviet Republic was a little too close to France though and eleven days later, French troops entered the region and put an end to this particular republic. Hungary and Slovakia were also governed by short-lived Soviet Republics in 1919.

The sudden desire to establish communist regimes in European countries manifested itself in the most unlikely locations. Switzerland has for many years been regarded as the absolute epitome of dull stability and yet there too the spectre of a Bolshevik uprising reared its head. On 2 August 1919, *The Times* reported that there had been fighting in the Swiss city of Basel, as an attempt was made to set up a Bolshevik power-base there. The paper went on to say that 'The government has taken energetic action, and a large number of troops were mobilised today, including cavalry, infantry, machine-gun corps, engineers and the staff of the Fourth Division. Armoured cars are patrolling the streets in the affected areas.' If Bolshevism could be causing such trouble even in the most notoriously peaceful country in Europe, then it was not surprising that the British government had apprehensions that their own country might not be immune to the revolutionary fervour which was sweeping westwards from Russia.

In 1918, British forces landed in North Russia to prevent military supplies there from falling into the hands of the Bolsheviks who now, nominally at least, were running the country. Outside the main cities of Moscow and Petrograd (present-day St. Petersburg), there was a good deal of chaos and as is so often the case with a collapsing empire, other nations thought that they might be able to seize portions of the disintegrating empire for themselves. Some members of the Cabinet in London, most notably Winston Churchill, believed that the fairly limited objectives of the forces in North Russia should be expanded and that an attempt should be made to 'strangle' the fledgling Bolshevik state at birth. Speaking many years later, in 1949, Churchill said: 'The failure to strangle Bolshevism at its birth and to bring Russia, prostrate, by one means or another, into the general democratic system lies heavy upon us today.'

With Marxism, in the form of Bolshevism, apparently spreading across

Europe in Britain's direction, Churchill and others in the Cabinet felt that the time was ripe to organise a crusade against Lenin's government. In an absolutely perfect textbook instance of the law of unintended consequences, this move, designed of course to neutralise the influence of Russian Bolshevism on the working classes of Britain, actually achieved the polar opposite, acting as a catalyst for some of the most serious disturbances ever seen in this country and bringing Britain to the brink of revolution. These problems, which reached unprecedented proportions, began in the army and spread outwards until they appeared at one point likely to engulf the entire country.

Lloyd George showed himself to be more prescient than his colleagues in the question of what, if anything, should be done about Russia. In a Cabinet meeting held on 31 December 1918, he made his own views clear, although he was later to bow to pressure from those who thought differently. He said, 'to send our soldiers to shoot down the Bolsheviks would be to create Bolsheviks here'. Despite this, the decision was made to send forces to Russia, although whether this actually constituted a war was never established. At the very least though, the adventures in the Baltic Sea and Arctic Ocean provided an excuse for delaying demobilisation, or at least slowing it down. To this extent, the invasion of Russia fitted in with Lloyd George's own ideas for avoiding or minimising the social upheaval which the country faced in 1919. Not that Lloyd George ever wanted or encouraged a military crusade against the newly-formed Bolshevik government in Russia; this was largely his Secretary of State for War Winston Churchill's own personal enterprise.

We shall, in Chapter 3, be looking at one final reason for delaying demobilisation and trying to keep as many men under arms as was possible. It was thought likely that the army would be needed not only to maintain order in distant parts of the Empire such as India and Mesopotamia, but also, when necessary, it might be called upon to control British workers and to enforce the will of the government upon an angry and discontented populace, either by breaking strikes or maintaining order on the streets. The army had, even before the war had ended, come very close to replacing the police as the guardians of public peace during the police strike of August 1918.

Less than three months after the signing of the Armistice in 1918, troops were indeed needed to patrol the streets of the second largest city in Britain, when the police proved unable to handle an outbreak of rioting.

17

But it was not necessary on that occasion for them to open fire, the very sight of their machine guns and tanks being enough to quell the disorder. It was claimed by a number of politicians that Britain came closer to revolution in 1919 and 1920 than at any other time in the country's history. Certainly, the scenes witnessed in this country during 1919 were quite unprecedented and nothing like them has ever been seen since.

In order to use the army to suppress strikes and tackle rioting though, it was necessary to know that they could be depended upon to follow instructions from officers. Whether the rank and file of the British Army would, when it came to it, obey orders, was by no means certain and as large-scale mutinies became increasingly common, the loyalty of sections of the army and navy was called into doubt. The fear in everybody's mind was what might happen if the army could no longer be relied upon. In the final analysis, the power and authority of any government, in Britain or elsewhere, rests on its ability to use overwhelming physical force against its enemies either at home or abroad. In 1919, it was looking as though the British government might no longer have the ability to command the unconditional loyalty of the armed forces.

Before looking at the alarming outbreaks of mutiny in the British armed forces in 1919, we must first examine the situation which served as the trigger for many of the insurrections. This was the possibility, one might even perhaps say threat, that conscripted men would be shipped off to the Arctic to take part in a civil war which was really no affair at all of Britain; the struggle between the Red Army and the Whites for the control of Russia.

Chapter 2

The British Invasion
of Russia

In the early spring of 1917, the German army was fighting Britain and France in the west and Russia in the east. Despite all the disadvantages of fighting simultaneously on two fronts, the Germans were holding their own and there was no present prospect of the war ending any time in the near future. When the Tsar was overthrown in February 1917, March by the Gregorian calendar used in the rest of the world, the natural and understandable fear of the British government was that the Russian Provisional Government would now make a separate peace with Germany, thus allowing the entire might of Germany to be unleashed upon the Western Front. This fear of Britain's was the fervent hope of the average Russian citizen; the nation was war-weary and exhausted after two-and-a-half years of the most gruelling and costly war which the world had ever seen. Fortunately for Britain and France, the new leader of Russia, Alexander Kerensky, was minded to fulfil his various obligations to foreign countries, even at the expense of his own people. He declared that Russia would continue to prosecute the increasingly unpopular war, a decision which would, before the year was out, lead to his fleeing Russia for refuge in the United States.

The war dragged on over the summer of 1917. In April, German U-boat attacks on neutral shipping brought America into the fighting on the side of the British and French. In Russia, the Bolsheviks agitated for the end of the war, under the seductive slogan of, 'Peace, Bread and Land'. It was perhaps the first of these three aims which struck the strongest chord among ordinary Russians. Discipline in the army collapsed and as autumn approached, officers were being shot by their men and units were refusing to advance across the whole of the front. Even without any agitation by forces opposed to the government, Russia's ability to wage war was evaporating by the day. By October, November in the rest of

Europe, Lenin and the Bolsheviks were ready. They struck at Kerensky's provisional government; seizing power in a brilliantly executed *coup d'état*.

Having promised peace, the Bolsheviks could hardly continue fighting. They announced a new policy, which was to be 'No peace, no war'. It was hoped that by simply stopping fighting, the Germans would leave Russia alone and concentrate their attentions on the British, American and French forces on the Western Front. However, scenting victory with one of the adversaries out of the fight, Germany reacted swiftly, threatening a major advance on the Eastern Front. Russia capitulated, signing the Treaty of Brest-Litovsk on 3 March 1918. This surrendered vast tracts of territory to Germany, along with much of Russia's population and industrial capacity. Faced with internal dissent, all that the Bolsheviks could hope to do to hang on to power in their own country: they were in no position at all to wage war against Germany, even had they been willing to abandon the pledges which they had made to gain the support of the Russian people.

To say that Britain, France and America were dismayed by this development, which they saw as rank treachery on the part of an ally, would be greatly to understate the case. Just three days after the Treaty of Brest-Litovsk was signed, the Royal Marines landed at Murmansk, a Russian port beyond the Arctic Circle. Their aim was, at least ostensibly, a limited and perfectly reasonable one. The British had shipped munitions to Murmansk to aid Russia in her war against Germany. Since the Russians had made peace with Germany, then they could scarcely have any further use for the weapons and ammunition which were now being stored in Murmansk. The British certainly did not wish to make a present to the Bolsheviks of this material and so thought that the easiest way of dealing with the problem would be simply to land and take everything back again.

It was this first action of the British armed forces against the Bolshevik government of Russia which began the train of events which some thought could have culminated in a revolution in Britain and the establishment there of a Soviet Republic, and so it might be an idea to put the British actions in context. There can be no doubt that Britain, France and America were all very put out with Russia in the spring of 1918. The British and French felt betrayed by an ally and feared that this betrayal would cost them dear in the lives of their soldiers in the months to come. France had an additional grudge in that the new Russian government had repudiated all its considerable debts to France. America also hated and distrusted the new regime, seeing in Bolshevism a dreadful scourge like some Biblical plague. The American Secretary of State Robert Lansing said, 'I can conceive of no more frightful calamity for a people than that which seems about to fall upon Russia.' For America, the new atheist government was ideologically objectionable, if nothing else.

Apart from the fairly reasonable and pragmatic motives which the British and French had for opposing Lenin's leadership of Russia, there was also the exciting prospect of an empire falling apart and the possibility of seizing some territory at it did so. The Japanese were first off the starting blocks in this particular race, landing forces at Vladivostok on Russia's Pacific coast on 5 April 1918. The avowed intention of this incursion was to protect any Japanese citizens living in Vladivostok. The real motive was to take for themselves the mineral-rich territory of Siberia. The Americans, not wishing to be left behind in the scramble, soon landed troops of their own at Vladivostok. As the Japanese moved west along the Trans-Siberian Railway, the French sent warships into the Black Sea, to menace Russia's unprotected southern flank.

Over the next few months, the British and Americans skirmished with Bolshevik forces and then, as a civil war broke out in Russia and it looked as though the Russians themselves would depose Lenin, the Allies decided to lend a hand, not only by supplying the 'Whites', those Russians who opposed the 'Reds', with money and arms, but also by joining in the fighting on their side. On 1 August 1918, Archangel, on the White Sea, was captured by combined British and American forces. By November, when the war in Europe was drawing to a close, Winston Churchill, Minister for Munitions in Lloyd George's government, had coined the expression, 'Kill the Bolshy, kiss the Hun!', which summed up what he saw as the priorities for the Allies after the end of the war against Germany. Churchill saw the Germans as being Britain's new friends in the struggle against the Bolshevik menace from the east.

The Armistice with Germany was signed on 11 November 1918. A few days earlier the Red Army had decided that it was time to eject the foreign troops from Archangel and Murmansk. Their efforts led to the Battle of Toulgas, which began on the very day that the Armistice was signed. It lasted for three days and resulted in defeat for the Bolsheviks.

The Red Army then turned its attention to the Baltic nation of Estonia, which was hoping to break free of Russia, invading the newly-independent country on 22 November. Soon, German and British soldiers were fighting side by side against the Red Army in defence of Estonia, and Churchill's idea of both kissing the 'Hun' and killing the 'Bolshy' became a reality. Even more assistance was rendered to Estonia on 31 December 1918, when a squadron of Royal Navy ships, under the command of Rear Admiral Sir Edwyn Alexander-Sinclair sailed into the Baltic. Having delivered a total of 6,500 rifles, 200 machine guns and two field guns to the Estonians for use against the Red Army, the British ships went into action against the Russian fleet. They captured the destroyers *Spartak* and *Avtroil* and promptly handed both ships over to the Estonians, who renamed them *Vambola* and *Lennuk*.

This then was the state of play in January 1919, when Lloyd George appointed Winston Churchill Secretary of State for War. The mood among the men who had been conscripted into the army was unequivocal; they wanted to be discharged immediately and allowed to return to their families. Churchill, though, had other ideas and these centred chiefly on eradicating Bolshevism from the world. For the first six months of the year, Lloyd George was mostly in France, sorting out the fine details of the peace treaty. This was unfortunate, because it gave his Secretary of State for War the opportunity to launch schemes aimed at dragging Britain further into various wars for which few people but he had any appetite.

It was generally recognised, not least by the Prime Minister himself, that Churchill had a bit of a bee in his bonnet where communism was concerned. This obsession coloured all his actions throughout 1919 and beyond. Frances Stevenson, who was Lloyd George's personal secretary, mistress and later wife, wrote shrewdly of Churchill at the time that, 'being Secretary of State for War, he is anxious that the world should not be at peace, & is therefore planning a great war in Russia', which summed the matter up neatly. Churchill himself said in a speech that year that, 'Of all the tyrannies in history the Bolshevik tyranny is the worst, the most destructive, and the most degrading.' Even the negotiations about the final settlement with Germany were, for Churchill, only of interest in as far as they had any bearing upon the fight against Bolshevism. He said that Britain should help Germany back onto its feet so that the Germans could help prevent the spread of Bolshevism. Little wonder then that Lloyd

George remarked openly at that time that Churchill had, 'Bolshevism on the brain.'

It was against this background that the mutinies in the British Army, at which we shall be looking in the next chapter, took place. At the signing of the Armistice in November 1918, millions of British men were under arms, the great majority of them conscripts. These men had spent years fighting Germany and now that they had achieved victory, wanted only to leave the army as soon as they could. This did not at all accord with Winston Churchill's view of the situation. Along with senior officer such as the Chief of the Imperial General Staff, General Sir Henry Wilson, Churchill had grand plans for Britain's role in the new world order.

When Britain went to war in August 1914, 733,514 men were serving in the British Army, all of them volunteers. By the beginning of 1919, when he was appointed Minister for War, it was quite clear to Churchill that such a relatively small army as that which had existed in 1914 would be quite inadequate for patrolling not only the British Empire, but also the various new territories which had been acquired during the war. At least twice as many men would be needed and if they could not be found by voluntary recruitment, then it would be necessary to retain some of those who had been conscripted from 1916 onwards.

While Lloyd George was in France in the early part of 1919, Churchill devised a plan which would establish a standing army of 1,150,000 men. These would be compulsorily retained in the army, the compulsion being sweetened by awarding them increased leave and greater pay. Those men who had enlisted before 31 December 1915, all those over the age of 37 and anybody with three or more wound stripes, could be demobilised immediately. So too would some who were so-called 'pivotal men', having important jobs to go back to. Having put together this scheme, Churchill then presented it to members of the Cabinet, without telling the Prime Minister what he was up to. This, not unnaturally, annoyed Lloyd George, although he later agreed to the idea. It was politically sensitive, because the government had been returned to power in December 1918, on what most people understood to be a promise of rapid demobilisation for all those who had been conscripted.

Lloyd George suspected, quite correctly, that Churchill was intriguing against him in the months after he had been given the post of Secretary of State for War. For much of the time, he was doing his best to embroil Britain in a war with Russia, which would have been disastrous for the government. Few in the Cabinet had any enthusiasm for the Bolshevik regime in Russia, but they could see what Churchill evidently could not, that the only practical consequence of a military crusade against Bolshevism would be to stimulate the growth of left-wing extremism in Britain itself. So it proved, for in January 1919 the National Committee for the Hands off Russia Campaign was elected in London. This was a pressure group consisting largely of communists and socialists. Harry Pollit, later to be the General Secretary of the Communist Party of Great Britain for almost thirty years, was a member, as were various other well-known left-wingers. The Hands off Russia Campaign drew public attention to the actions which British forces were taking in the Arctic and Baltic.

Britain had already been militarily involved in Russian affairs before Churchill came to the War Office and even in 1918 there had been murmurs of discontent about what was happening. These concerns were not limited to a handful of left-wing rabble-rousers in London. Ominously, the first stirrings of mutiny had begun in the navy, where sailors were showing a marked reluctance to be shipped north as the war with Germany ended, so that they could be thrown into battle against a new enemy. In the summer of 1918, there was unrest among sailors of the Royal Navy, not only about the prospect of being sent to Russia, by also about the more mundane and practical issues of pay and conditions on board their ships. George Lambert, Liberal MP for South Molton, referred to this in a speech to the House of Commons on 12 March 1919, saying, 'But undoubtedly there was at the end of last year grave unrest in the navy . . . I do not want to be violent but I think I am correct in saying that a match would have touched an explosion.'

It is perhaps significant that there had been no mutinies in the Royal Navy throughout the whole of the First World War and that the first problems coincided with the decision to send the navy into the Baltic and up to the Arctic. Soon after the signing of the Armistice in November 1918, the crew of a British light cruiser anchored at the Latvian port of Libau mutinied and refused to sail. There were similar problems on a lesser scale with ships at Archangel and Murmansk. During the war, such actions would have put men in hazard of facing a firing squad, but there was no desire at all to execute any members of the British forces now that the Armistice had been signed.

In January 1919, the Admiralty were warned that attempts were being made to start a trade union for sailors, one which would have the power to call a strike if grievances were ignored. Of course, a 'strike' in the armed forces is simply another word for 'mutiny' and the Admiralty moved quickly to try and stop the idea getting any further. The best way of doing so was to see what the sailors were complaining of and how far it might be possible to placate them by improving things. Rear Admiral Sir Thomas Jerram was given the task of touring British ports to talk to the men and listen to their grievances.

Raising pay was one thing which could be done, but only the government in London could countermand orders to sail for Russian waters. It was this, the orders to hazard their lives to engage the forces of a former ally, that many ordinary seamen really objected to. On 13 January 1919, the gunboat HMS *Kilbride* was stationed at Milford Haven, when the crew simply refused to obey orders and, in an alarming echo of the Russian battleship *Potemkin* in 1905, raised the red flag. That same month saw the crews of other ships at Invergordon, Rosyth, Devonport and Portsmouth refusing to weigh anchor and sail for action against Russia.

The men already in the Baltic and White Seas were also growing mutinous. HMS *Cicala*, a 645-ton gunboat, had been ordered to sail up the River Dvina, exposing the ship to fire from Bolshevik batteries on the banks of the river. This was too much for the majority of the crew, who refused to sail. Admiral Cowan, in charge of the vessel, threatened to use force and eventually managed to restore order. However, the admiral was uncertain whether these mutineers were actually refusing to obey officers in the face of the enemy. He contacted the Admiralty in London, who in turn consulted the Cabinet. The question to which Admiral Cowan sought an answer was a simple and straightforward one; was Britain at war with the Bolsheviks? The answer, sanctioned by the Prime Minister himself, came back informing Admiral Cowan that he should indeed consider the forces under his command to be at war. Five of the ringleaders of the mutiny were accordingly sentenced to death, but this was later commuted to five years' imprisonment.

Although there were other causes of dissatisfaction among members of Britain's armed forces, things such as low rates of pay and the desire for more speedy demobilisation, there can be no doubt that it was the prospect of being sent to fight in Russia which was the decisive factor in triggering many of the mutinies seen in 1919. The government had announced, for public consumption, the untruthful statement that only volunteers would be sent to Russia. It was to draw attention to the fact that they were being coerced into sailing north that many of the mutinies were launched in 1919 by men who just wanted to stop fighting and return to their families. Mutiny in the navy was bad enough, but there was at least the hope that it could be kept quiet, especially when it took place in a remote corner of the Arctic. News of mutiny in one place can precipitate mutiny in others and that was the last thing anybody wished to see. The real trouble came when the mutinies began in the army. That some of these took place in big cities such as Dover, Southampton and even London, made it a racing certainty that word would spread about what had happened and that the news would soon get around that the British Army could no longer be depended upon to obey orders.

Chapter 3

Mutiny in the Armed Forces

It is not often that one is able to pinpoint precisely the moment when a war is lost or won, nor the hour in which a revolution becomes successful and the existing regime overthrown. In the case of the Russian Revolution, we know the exact moment that the downfall of the Romanovs, who had ruled Russia for over three centuries, was assured without the shadow of a doubt. It happened early on the morning of Monday 12 March 1917.

During the days approaching this fateful date, the troops of the Imperial Army had shown a marked reluctance to act against the crowds of strikers and demonstrators who thronged the streets of Petrograd, the modern-day city of St Petersburg. Even the Cossacks, the traditional means in Russia of dispersing crowds of discontented citizenry, had refused to ride down the protesters, let alone draw their sabres and attack them. They would not even wield their whips against the people of Petrograd. So far, the armed forces had displayed passive disobedience, rather than engaging in open mutiny. This all changed abruptly on that Monday morning, when a certain Sergeant Timofeyef Kirpichnikov marched the Volinsk Regiment from its barracks in good order, with the band playing, through the streets of Petrograd to the barracks of the Preobrazhensky and Litovsky Regiments, where he called upon them to join his men in fighting against the established order and throw in their lot with the rebellious crowds of strikers and unemployed workers. As soon as the Tsar and his government could no longer rely upon the army to obey orders, they were in desperate straits. On the day that a body of troops declared themselves to be actively opposed to the existing regime; the Russian leadership were altogether lost.

Mutiny in the armed forces has always been treated with great severity in Britain. The death penalty for murder was abolished in the 1960s, but it was to be another 30 years before those convicted of mutiny were freed from the possibility of being sentenced to death. It was not until 1998 that this offence ceased to attract the ultimate penalty in this country. The reason is easy to understand. The power of any government rests in the final analysis in the ability to use overwhelming force to impose its will, either upon the country it governs or against other nations with whom it may be at war. As Mao Zedong observed, 'Political power grows from the barrel of a gun'. If your soldiers conspire together to disobey the orders of superior officers, so that you can no longer rely upon them to do as you wish, then you have really lost your ability to govern in any meaningful sense of the word. It is for this reason that mutiny has traditionally been seen as being on a par with treason; it strikes against the very authority of the state. This was the position in which the government of Lloyd George found itself as 1919 began. It could no longer rely unconditionally upon the loyalty of the armed forces and, just as in Russia in 1917, there was a very real chance of units transferring their allegiance to an authority other than the Crown.

Before going further, it might be helpful to explore in a little detail the position of soldiers and police officers in the United Kingdom. All civil servants, army officers, police constables and government ministers in Britain owe their allegiance not to the Prime Minister or any other political figure, but to the Crown. The same of course goes for the Prime Minister himself. This loyalty filters down from above and is the ultimate source of authority upon which all public servants rely. The Prime Minister is an agent of the Crown and it is in this capacity that he instructs his Minister of Defence, who then tells the military commanders what is required. They in turn pass on orders to their subordinates, all the way down to junior officers and NCOs, who are in charge of the ordinary soldiers and sailors. At each stage, the ministers, civil servants and officers are acting not in a personal capacity, according to their own whims and fancies, nor as followers of this or that political party, but rather as conduits for the authority of the Crown. In this respect, a strike by police officers or disobedience by soldiers is of a qualitatively different nature to industrial action by workers in a factory or mine. Setting oneself in opposition to an employer is not to be compared with rebelling against the Crown.

Throughout 1919, first the army and then the police suffered from what, on the face of it, appeared to be merely a tendency to strike and oppose the authority of their superiors in a way which was superficially similar and to some observers indistinguishable from the wave of militant

28

action bedevilling industry at that time. However, a railway worker going on strike may still maintain his loyalty to the state or the Crown; he is just engaged in a dispute with his bosses about wages and working conditions. Such strikes can be an awful nuisance, but do not necessarily represent a challenge to the established order, although of course some do. When soldiers elect their own committees though and, rejecting the orders of their officers, follow the instructions issued by their own representatives, something very different is going on. These are men who have rejected the power of the state, as embodied by the Crown, and are moving off into the territory of creating their own alternative state, whether they realise it or not. The same is true of striking police officers, which is of course why it is illegal for the British police to go on strike or even belong to a trade union, a state of affairs which arose as direct consequence of the events in 1919.

Mutiny, the rebellion of soldiers against their superiors, had been a negligible problem in European armies at the beginning of the First World War. As the years passed though, it grew to such serious levels that two of the major participants in the war, Russia and Germany, were forced to stop fighting, simply because their armies would no longer go to war when told to do so. The French army had enormous difficulties with large-scale mutiny in the latter half of the war, which they only manage to suppress by conducting thousands of courts martial. In the summer of 1917, for example, 3,427 courts martial were held for mutiny, which resulted in 629 sentences of death, although only forty-three of these were actually carried out. In the final year of the war, there were over 20,000 cases of mutiny in the French army and if the war had continued for much longer, it is entirely possible that France too might have found itself in the same unenviable situation as Germany and Russia.

There had been odd cases of mutiny in the British Army in France during the First World War, but they were freakishly rare, resulting in only a tiny handful of executions, compared with the over 300 soldiers who were shot for cowardice, desertion and other military offences. It was not until the war had technically ended that mutiny became so widespread as to longer appear at all remarkable. The first of these post-war mutinies took place at an army base in the Sussex seaside town of Shoreham. Before looking at the mutinies of 1919, we should note that mutiny in the British Army was traditionally a random and haphazard business, consisting of individuals or small groups of men rebelling spontaneously against their NCOs and officers. Such outbreaks of indiscipline, while prejudicial to good order in the army or navy, were fairly easy to deal with. The peaceful and organised mutinies of 1919 were another matter entirely.

Dissatisfaction about the demobilisation of those who had been conscripted into the army began within 48 hours of the signing of the Armistice on 11 November 1918. This, the first mutiny to take place in the British Army after the end of the war against Germany, set a dangerous precedent which was to have serious consequences over the coming year. On 13 November, a major at the camp in Shoreham had abused a conscripted man and then pushed him into some mud. This was enough to cause almost every soldier at Shoreham, of whom the vast majority were conscripts, to rebel. A mass walkout was organised and the men made it plain that they would not be obeying orders and felt that now that the war had ended, they should be released at once from the army. Over 7,000 men marched the six miles to Brighton Town Hall, in perfect order and without any officers supervising them, and held a rally there. The gist of their demands was that they should be demobilised at once, as the war was now over. Both the Chief Constable and the Mayor, Alderman Herbert Carden JP, met the soldiers and the Mayor made a speech from the balcony of the Town Hall, telling the troops that he agreed with them and would contact the government on their behalf. The next day, a general was sent from London to talk to the men and issue orders which he hoped would be followed without question. They were not and not one of the men did as they had been ordered and returned to their posts. The official response to this mutiny of thousands of soldiers was simply astonishing. The day after the general had visited the camp, a thousand of the men were demobilised. More were released over the following days. The message seemed to be very clear: it paid to mutiny. This immediate and ill thought-out response to an unexpected crisis sent quite the wrong signal to other conscripts hoping to be sent home soon. It seemed that organised opposition to officers would be rewarded with demobilisation!

In December 1918, the United Kingdom's first general election for eight years was held. It had been delayed by the onset of war in 1914, but with the signing of the Armistice, there could be no excuse for Lloyd George not going to the country. Conscious of the public mood regarding the continuation of conscription, Lloyd George made public statements which were interpreted by many as a promise to demobilise all conscripted men as speedily as possible. General Sir Henry Wilson, Chief of the Imperial General Staff and overall head of the British Army, was horrified. He already had plans for armies of occupation, consisting mainly of conscripts, to be sent to France, India and elsewhere. This was to say nothing of the new commitment to the military adventure in northern Russia. Writing in his diary in 1919, when mutiny had become practically a way of life for the army, Wilson said, 'The whole trouble is due to Lloyd George and his cursed campaign for vote catching'.

Lloyd George had been re-elected as Prime Minister and was, at the beginning of 1919, agonising about the best way to deal with demobilisation and the possible end to conscription. Meanwhile, Wilson had found an ally within the Cabinet, a man who, like him, wished to topple the Bolshevik regime in Russia and at the same time maintain an enormous army which would police the world. Winston Churchill, later to lead Britain to victory during the Second World War, was appointed Secretary of State for War in Lloyd George's new administration. He at once set about frustrating any attempt to rapidly demobilise the conscripted troops. In secret meetings with the Chief of the Imperial General Staff, Churchill laid plans that the two men would later that year present to the Prime Minister as a *fait accompli*.

A great cause of anger among the conscripted men was the grossly unfair way that demobilisation was being managed. In an effort to avoid flooding the country with unemployed men, the government adopted a scheme which allowed for the immediate discharge of what were called 'pivotal' men; those who already had jobs to go to in important branches of trade and industry. Because there had been a deliberate system of not calling up men doing 'pivotal' jobs until it was really necessary, these tended to be conscripts who had been in the army for just a few months, some having been drafted only during the Ludendorff Offensive in the spring of 1918. This was a time when every man was needed to contain the German advance; which at one point threatened even the Channel ports of Belgium and France. Clearly, now that the crisis was over, then the sooner such men were released to go back to important jobs which had been kept open for them, the better.

This policy meant that demobilisation was, in effect, being conducted on the basis of 'last in, first out', which was obviously unjust. Men who had been called up in the spring of 1916 and then endured the horrors of

31

the Somme and Passchendaele were being kept in the army, while others who had been conscripted only a month or two before were allowed to return to civilian life. The sheer, monstrous injustice of this absurd situation helped to provoke one of the most extensive mutinies that the British Army had ever known. It took place not on some distant battlefield, but in the Kent port of Folkestone.

A number of soldiers who had been on active service in France were granted leave so that they could return to England to be with their families over Christmas and the New Year. Many of these men understood that once back in Britain, they would then be demobilised. Lloyd George's electioneering speeches helped to confirm them in this view. To their amazement, after their leave ended, instead of being demobilised they were ordered to return to France. Worse still, rumours began circulating to the effect that some of them were to be shipped off to the Arctic to fight what Winston Churchill described in a speech at the Mansion House in London that year as the 'foul baboonery' of Bolshevism.

The majority of the thousands of men who arrived at Folkestone harbour, where they were due to board ships to France, were in a sullen and uncooperative mood. On 3 January, the simmering tensions exploded and, in perfect discipline, 2,000 soldiers took over the port and announced that no military vessels would be allowed to sail. Pickets were posted on the dockside and as troop trains reached Folkestone, they were met by representatives of the troops who had brought the port to a standstill and invited to join them. Most did so and by the next morning, Saturday 4 January, something in the region of 10,000 soldiers were running their own affairs without officers and patrolling the quayside to ensure that no boats sailed for either France or Russia.

There could hardly have been a more alarming situation; either for the government in London or the commanders of the army. This was no undisciplined rabble on the rampage, but thousands of men peacefully setting up their own committees and refusing to obey any orders unless they came from the men they had themselves chosen to lead them. It was in fact, precisely what had happened in Russia when the army changed sides and refused any longer to support the monarchy and also later when they followed the advice of their own soviets, rather than the orders of the Provisional Government in Petrograd. Already, there were fears about the mood of the country's industrial workers, strikes were running at a record high, and the well-founded apprehension was that these disaffected and mutinous soldiers might make common cause with rebellious workers.

A half-hearted effort to stamp out the mutiny by the use of force failed miserably. A squad of Fusiliers under the command of an officer took up position at the dockside with fixed bayonets and their rifles loaded. As they were approached by some of the mutineers, one of the Fusiliers raised his rifle, as though about to fire. He evidently thought better of it though, because the scene passed off peacefully. The Commander-in-Chief of Home Forces, General Sir William Robertson, was driven from London to Folkestone and promised the men that there would be no reprisals for their actions and that their leave would be extended. Once again, the staging of a mutiny appeared to have reaped rich rewards for the soldiers involved. Little wonder that the trouble then spread to the nearby port of Dover, where again, additional leave was granted.

It must have seemed to the conscripted men who were organising these protests that the authorities were weak and ready to concede to demands they made. On 6 January, the trouble reached Downing Street itself. Men of the Army Service Corps, based at Isleworth just outside London, had heard that their regiment was likely to be one of the last to be demobilised. They commandeered lorries and drove to Downing Street to protest in person to the Prime Minister. When they arrived at Downing Street, which they blocked with their lorries, it was to find that Lloyd George was not there and so they discussed their concerns with civil servants from the Ministry of Labour. Four days later, many of them were demobilised.

The generals could see the army melting away before their eyes, such was the reaction of a government which was anxious at all costs to avoid any violent confrontation. Other mutinies took place over the course of the next few weeks at camps in various parts of Southern England. Although he hoped to resolve the crisis without bloodshed, the Prime Minister must have known that he could not let this sort of thing continue unchecked. Even if he did not fully agree with Wilson's estimate of the numbers of troops needed to run the British Empire effectively, Lloyd George was keenly aware that he was likely very soon to need large numbers of soldiers upon whom he could rely absolutely to obey orders. These would be operating not in India or Mesopotamia, but in Britain itself and unless he could be sure of their loyalty, then the country faced its greatest test since the end of the English Civil War, almost 300 years earlier.

It is sometimes forgotten that for most of British history the guardians of public peace have been not the police, but the army. Even after the establishment of the first police forces in this country during the nineteenth century, the army's role in maintaining order was crucial. Whenever the police found themselves unable to handle anything from riots to peaceful gatherings of striking textile workers, then the magistrates in an area could, and frequently did, enlist the aid of the army in crushing anything which appeared to smack to the authorities of rebellion or sedition. At the beginning of 1919, this role of the armed forces was no historical curiosity: one didn't need a long memory to see what role the army was expected to play when things threatened to get out of hand. It was only necessary to look back to the terrible events of 1911, the year that saw what became known as the 'Great Unrest'.

During 1911, over a million workers came out on strike in Britain. Transport workers, seamen, dockers, miners and railwaymen were all on strike at various times and the government resorted to the time-honoured expedient of calling out the military to deal with the strikes and riots which were plaguing the country. In August, a national strike of seamen began and in the northern port of Liverpool, thousands of other workers laid down their tools in sympathy. Almost 100,000 strikers filled the streets and, fearing that they were facing the beginning of large-scale disorders, the authorities arranged for the Riot Act to be read and then cavalry were used to clear the streets. In the resulting riot, windows were smashed, fires started and barricades erected. The following day, armoured cars and soldiers with fixed bayonets patrolled the streets. Reinforcements were brought in from nearby army bases and within 48 hours, some 3,500 soldiers had taken control of public order in Liverpool and the city was virtually under martial law.

Just as in the aftermath of the rioting in English cities in 2011, it was thought that a few lengthy sentences for public order offences might discourage future episodes of disorder. Some of the men arrested during the initial street fighting were taken to court and given stiff terms of imprisonment. A detachment of thirty hussars were given the task of escorting the vans taking the prisoners from the magistrates' court to Walton Prison. As they passed through the streets, angry crowds gathered; perhaps with the intention of rescuing the men being taken off to prison. A few daring protestors grabbed at the reins of the cavalry troopers, whereupon an officer gave the order to open fire. Two men were killed and another three wounded. Michael Prendegast, one of those killed, had been shot twice through the head.

Incredibly, the violence in Liverpool was not the worst to be seen in Britain that summer. Troops also opened fire at Llanelli in Wales. During the resulting fighting, which included saboteurs setting fire to a railway truck containing explosives, six people were killed. Tredegar, also in Wales, saw the first anti-Jewish pogrom in Britain since the Middle Ages. Once again, the army was called in to restore order, elements of the Somerset Light Infantry and the Worcester Regiment making bayonet charges along the streets of the town. Cavalry were also used to drive off looters and those intent upon burning shops. London itself became an armed camp, with 12,500 soldiers billeted in tents in Hyde Park. Troops guarded railway stations and patrolled the lines leading in and out of London. The fear was that sabotage might be attempted. Without the assistance of the army, it is unlikely that the police alone would have been able to deal effectively with the situation that year.

This then was another great fear of Lloyd George and his government at the beginning of 1919; that social unrest and industrial action might increase to such a level that the police would be unable to cope with the situation. In the usual way of things, the army would at this point have been brought in to help, but it was becoming increasingly clear that many units simply could not be relied upon to obey orders. As if that was not a disturbing-enough possibility, it was also the case that the police themselves might not do as they were told by the authorities. There had already been one police strike in 1918 and the signs were that another might be on the way. If the police walked out and the army refused to act, what would become of the country?

Just before the outbreak of war in 1914, a police trade union had been formed, the National Union of Police and Prison Officers (NUPPO). By 1918, this union had become strong enough to call a strike of police officer in London. Twelve thousand Metropolitan Police officers, the majority of the force, walked out in a dispute over various issues, including pay. Troops were deployed at key positions across London and Prime Minister Lloyd George gave in to nearly all the demands made by the striking officers. In the event of another such strike, the army might not be available to act. There were those in the Cabinet who were beginning to think that the country was facing a Bolshevik revolution, like that which had seized power in Russia.

Also at the forefront of Lloyd George's mind must have been events in Germany, both in November 1918 and also on the very day that the men of the Army Service Corps seized lorries and drove to London to try and confront him. The downfall of Germany's Kaiser was caused by mutinies in the army and navy. It was when he realised that he was no longer in control of Germany's armed forces that Kaiser Wilhelm knew that the game was up and that he no longer held power, just as had been the case with Tsar Nicholas the previous year. The army and navy were the key to the continued existence or overthrow of any regime.

On 6 January 1919, the same day that the discontented soldiers arrived in Downing Street to demand immediate demobilisation, an abortive revolution erupted in Berlin. Vast crowds gathered and were addressed by members of the Spartacist movement; later to be renamed the German Communist Party. A number of public buildings were occupied and one of the Spartacist leaders, Karl Liebknecht, proclaimed the creation of the German Soviet Republic. Red flags were raised across the city. The German communists were hoping to emulate the Bolshevik seizure of Russia, when the weak Provisional Government which took power after the Tsar's abdication was itself overthrown.

As always, the army was the key to the whole thing and if the German army had not been loyal to the newly-formed republic which had taken power in November 1918, then it is possible that Germany would indeed have seen the establishment of a 'Dictatorship of the Proletariat', as Lenin had instituted in Russia. As it was, not only did the army stand firmly on the side of the republic, a number of right-wing militias were not prepared to stand by and see the country taken over by Marxists. Over the following days, the communists were routed and then hunted down and killed. It was a one-sided contest, for those who were opposed to them had machine guns and artillery at their disposal. On 15 January, just nine days after the proclamation of the Soviet Republic, Karl Liebknecht was killed.

The message from Germany's experience could scarcely be clearer. As long as the army were on the side of the government, then that government were secure; no matter what a handful of troublemakers and malcontents might do. The difficulty for the government in London was that it was looking as though their army was not altogether on the right side and if a firm line was not taken soon, then the British Army was in danger of crumbling away as a force to be reckoned with. This was a terrifying prospect and perhaps explains why the next time that an organised mutiny took place, there was no question of acceding to the demands of the men. Instead, the gloves would be off and it would be made plain that those who disobeyed orders would find themselves in very serious trouble; even their very lives would be in danger.

It was not long before the opportunity arose to demonstrate this new resolve. It came in the middle of January, when over 5,000 soldiers in the port of Southampton went on strike, as they saw it. Of course, there can really be no such thing as a strike in the army and by any definition, what was really happening was simply a mutiny. The soldiers took over the Southampton docks and it was observed that the inhabitants of the city appeared to be in sympathy with them. The main complaint being made was that the soldiers had understood that they had been told to report to Southampton so that they could be demobilised. Now, though, they were being ordered to board ships for France. This was a point of view which was bound to generate sympathy among the residents of Southampton, almost all of whom had husbands, brothers and fathers in the same position. This is just what had happened during the mutinies in Dover and Folkestone – ordinary people seemed to agree with the grievances of the troops and behaved as though they wished to support and encourage the mutinies. When it became apparent that the same pattern was developing in Southampton, General Sir William Robertson, who had negotiated a peaceful resolution to the trouble in Folkestone, knew that unless he acted firmly, there would soon be no soldiers upon whom he could rely to obey orders unconditionally. Instead of travelling down to Southampton and talking reasonably with the men about their demands, Robertson sent a general down to deal with the mutiny in any way he saw fit. The man chosen to tackle the mutiny at Southampton was General Hugh Trenchard, former commander of the Royal Flying Corps and later appointed Commissioner of the Metropolitan Police. He had been taking a two-month holiday following the Armistice, and was specifically recalled to active service to handle the Southampton mutiny in such a way as to send a clear signal to the rest of the conscripts in the armed forces that this sort of thing would no longer be tolerated.

Trenchard was a career soldier who had received his first commission in 1893, at the height of Britain's imperial power. He was a man who had for almost thirty years been used to others leaping to obey him when he issued orders. When he received the telegram instructing him to go down to the south coast, General Trenchard put on his uniform and set off in the expectation that only a few sharp words from a very senior officer would be enough to nip this nonsense in the bud. He had had experience of mutinies in France and knew that in most cases it was simply one or two barrack-room-lawyer types egging on others to disregard authority. This is how the army traditionally saw mutiny: a small number of ringleaders urging on the more weak-minded of their fellows to follow a ruinous course of action.

On reaching Southampton, Trenchard had a brief interview with the commander of the camp where the troops had been stationed. He formed the view that he was an indecisive and ineffective man, who had by his vacillation allowed a minor problem to snowball into a crisis. As the General had suspected all along, all that was needed was for a man of action to go and speak firmly to the men and the whole business would be over in a matter of minutes. Accompanied only by his aide-de-camp Maurice Baring and a clerk, Trenchard set off for the docks.

When he approached the dock gates and demanded to be allowed in to address the thousands of soldiers who were occupying the area, it did not once occur to General Trenchard that he would be received with anything other than the respect due to a senior officer. He was sadly mistaken, because as soon as they caught sight of his uniform, the boos, catcalls and angry shouting began. To his utmost amazement, the abuse escalated from the verbal to the physical. He was grabbed and roughly manhandled, before being ignominiously ejected from the docks. Many years later, Trenchard still recalled with disbelief the treatment he had received: 'It was the only time in my life I had been really hustled. They did not want to listen to me. They told me to get out and stay out.' Seething with fury, he went off and telephoned the garrison commander at nearby Portsmouth, demanding that he be sent 250 armed troops and also an escort of military police. The men occupying the docks were all unarmed, which Trenchard knew. He had resolved to teach them a lesson for their atrocious conduct, if need be by instigating a massacre.

Trenchard's request for urgent military assistance had set alarm bells ringing in the higher echelons of the army in southern England. In the middle of the night, Trenchard was called to the telephone to take a call from the General Officer in charge of the Southern Command. This man informed him that under no circumstances must Trenchard give the order to open fire in Southampton. Since he outranked this officer, Trenchard merely informed him coldly that he was not seeking anybody's permission for what he was about to do.

The next day, Trenchard was waiting at the station for the troop train to arrive from Portsmouth. When the soldiers he had requested had disembarked, they were ordered to load their rifles and fix bayonets. These were instructions which, in the usual way of things, were only issued before a battle was about to commence. The soldiers were then marched to the docks. Most of the mutineers had spent the night in the customs hall, a huge barn-like structure with an open front. Trenchard drew up his men and then ordered them to cock their weapons and to be prepared to fire on the word of command. Nobody present had the least doubt that the general who had been humiliated by the men in the custom hall was perfectly ready to initiate a bloodbath if he did not get his way. Once more, Trenchard began to address the crowd. A sergeant shouted an obscenity and was immediately seized by the military police. The overwhelming force was effective and all but 100 men holed up in some buildings agreed to surrender. At Trenchard's command, the windows were smashed and men who had barricaded themselves in the buildings had fire hoses turned on them until they too capitulated. The mutiny was over. Trenchard personally identified those who he thought were ringleaders and they were taken off in the custody of the military police. In February, when Trenchard was summoned to London and offered by Winston Churchill the post of Chief of the Air Staff, Churchill, who was by now both Secretary of State for War and also Secretary of State for Air, congratulated him on his actions, referring to Trenchard's 'masterly handling' of the 'Southampton riots'.

Towards the end of January, the War Office sent a circular stamped 'Secret' to all commanding officers throughout the United Kingdom. This secret document revealed the deepest anxieties of the government in London, showing precisely why they wished to be sure of the mood of various units of the armed forces. Because of the mutinies which had been taking place, it was hoped to discover how many troops would actually be likely to obey any orders to come to the aid of the civil power. The officers were to furnish Whitehall with weekly reports, to arrive 'not later than first post each Thursday morning', telling the War Office which units could be relied upon in a domestic crisis of the sort which was expected that year. Among the questions were:

• Will troops in various areas respond to orders for assistance to preserve the public peace?
• Will they assist in strike-breaking?
• Will they parade for draft to overseas, especially to Russia?

There were also questions about outside agitation, the growth of trade unionism and the formation of soldiers' councils. No sooner had the circular been issued, than another mutiny took place at the British bases at the Channel port of Calais. This was an even worse situation than the ones which had been seen in Southern England that year. Men from the Royal Army Ordnance Corps and the Army Service Corps were refusing to operate the ports and had joined forces with French workers to bring the railways and shipping to a halt. At the same time, units of front-line troops waiting at Calais refused to obey orders. The men involved described their actions as a 'strike', but since they were paralysing one of the key ports being used by the British Army and preventing the movement of both troops and military supplies to the army currently stationed on the German border, it was clear that their actions were jeopardising the whole of Britain's efforts on the Continent.

The rebel forces, for there is really no other way to describe them, had formed a committee to run both their own affairs and also to take control of the port of Calais. This organisation, the Calais Soldiers' and Sailors' Association, was effectively controlling thousands of British troops in the camps around Calais. The demands of the men on 'strike' varied from improvements in rations to speedier demobilisation. It is impossible to say just how many men were actually taking part in this episode, estimates ranging from 4,000 to 20,000, as well as French railway workers who were refusing to assist in the movement of British troop trains and so on.

After the mutinies which had been seen in England and the ill effects of leniency on those actively involved, Commander-in-Chief of the British forces in France, Field Marshal Sir Douglas Haig, was not in the mood for compromise. All else apart, Germany was not yet, despite the Armistice, technically defeated and there existed the possibility that if a satisfactory peace treaty could not be put together, then the British and French armies would be forced to invade Germany. In such a case, the Channel ports would be of crucial importance from a logistical point of view. Haig sent orders to General Sir Julian Byng, commander of the

Third Army, authorising him to move two divisions to Calais and put an end to the mutiny by any means necessary.

Byng's arrival in Calais on 27 January was delayed because of the strikes which French railway workers were undertaking in support of the British mutineers. When he and the two divisions which Haig had allocated for this matter reached Calais, Byng showed that he was in no mood for pussyfooting around, surrounding the camps which were at the centre of the mutiny and having his men set up machine-gun positions. He then gave the men a straight choice. If they wished to make a fight of it, then he and his troops would oblige. Otherwise, they should lay down their arms and surrender. Having threatened to deal with the mutiny by the use of overwhelming military force, Byng had four men whom he regarded as the ringleaders arrested and sent for court martial. Then he arranged for improvements in the conditions in the camps. Haig wished to make an example of the men who organised what was called by some of those who set it up the 'Calais Soviet'. Specifically, he wished to see them shot for mutiny. Secretary of State for War Winston Churchill overruled the C-in-C, though, and the four men were instead sentenced to long terms of imprisonment.

By now, Lloyd George's government was facing another crisis, this time on the industrial front and they needed to ensure that at least some of the army would help deal with what had come to resemble a Bolshevik revolution in the Scottish city of Glasgow. Acting on the advice of Wilson, Lloyd George had recalled to Britain some units of the Guards, whose loyalty was unquestionable. Many of the men in the five Guards regiments were volunteers from before the war and would obey orders without hesitation. They comprised at that time the Grenadier Guards, the Coldstream Guards, the Scots Guards, the Welsh Guards and the Irish Guards. It was vital to have such soldiers at the command of the government, because the country now faced a serious confrontation with strikers in important industries. The government believed, quite correctly, that these strikes were about more than the usual demands for shorter hours and higher pay. It was felt necessary to have troops ready to crush the strikers, by any means which might be needed.

Bringing the Guards back to Britain was intended in part as a show of force for those who were seeking to destabilise the country and, in some cases, conspiring to overthrow the established order. Lest this appear fanciful, we turn to the memoirs of an officer who served in the First

World War and went on to become a respected academic and author. Charles Carrington's biography of Rudyard Kipling is still, sixty years after its publication, regarded as being the authoritative work on the subject. In 1963, Carrington published *Soldier from the War Returning*, an account of his own experiences during and shortly after the war. He describes a parade through central London after some units of the Guards had been brought back to Britain: '. . . the Guards Division was brought home from France and paraded through London in fighting order, ostensibly to allow the Londoners to welcome their own familiar defenders, and with a secondary motive of warning the seditious that force would be met with force . . . It was a celebration, and at the same time a warning that there was still a disciplined army.'

In the event, the Guards were needed first not to tackle industrial unrest in the provinces, but in London itself. Before we examine in the next chapter the use of troops against strikers, which took place in Scotland in January 1919, it is instructive to see how the Guards came in handy when hundreds of heavily-armed soldiers descended on central London and needed to be dispersed by force. On Friday 7 February 1919, a large number of soldiers reported to Victoria Station. Some had thought that they were about to be demobilised, while others believed that they were to be sent to France. In the end, neither of these things happened. It had been intended that the men would board trains and then travel to the coast and from there to France. However, due to a mix-up, no trains were available. The men, mostly from the North of England, were told to make their own arrangements for the next few days and to report back at Victoria Station the next day. This caused a great deal of anger. Those who had thought that they might be discharged from the army that day were dismayed to hear that they would instead be sent overseas. Even the ones who were resigned to another posting in France were angry that they were expected to find food and lodgings for themselves in the capital that night. Many had no money and faced the prospect of sleeping in the waiting rooms at the station.

On the Saturday, matters became serious. There were still no available trains and no provision had been made for accommodation or food for the stranded soldiers. Tempers flared and there was scuffling and raised voices, the officers present bearing the brunt of the displeasure being freely expressed by the indignant soldiers. It was at this point that the value of recalling various detachments of Guards' regiments became obvious. Other units of conscripted men might have sympathised or even fraternised with the infuriated men. Not so the company of Scots Guards who were despatched from their barracks near Buckingham Palace. They marched to the station, halted long enough to fix bayonets and then cleared Victoria Station of civilians, isolating the rebellious troops in the station yard. These men were then surrounded and disarmed, being later taken under arrest to Wellington Barracks.

So chaotic and confused was the scene at Victoria Station, that the Scots Guards who were dealing with one group of soldiers in the station yard failed to realise that a large contingent were assembling elsewhere. When these other men saw that the Guards were intent upon disarming and arresting anybody protesting about the treatment they had received, they formed up into marching order and set off along Victoria Street in the direction of Parliament. The situation could hardly have been more fraught, however much the government later tried to play it down. Almost a thousand rebellious soldiers, all armed with rifles and ignoring their officers, were now marching on the Houses of Parliament. Word was sent to the War Ministry, where the Secretary of State for War was at his desk, despite its being a Saturday. The first thing that Churchill must have wondered was if this was the beginning of some kind of *coup d'état*. He telephoned Major-General Sir Geoffrey Feilding, who, in addition to commanding the Brigade of Guards, was General Officer Commanding London District. Since the Scots Guards were fully occupied at Victoria Station, Churchill wished to know what other units were available at that moment to deal with a new threat from mutinous troops. General Feilding told Churchill that he had at his disposal a reserve battalion of the Grenadier Guards and two troops of the Household Cavalry. It was at this point that the Secretary of State asked the all-important question: would these troops obey orders? General Feilding assured him that there was no doubt at all about their loyalty.

From the window of his office, Churchill could see the hundreds of soldiers, rifles at the slope, marching down Whitehall. Perhaps worried about the consequences if they saw the man who was in overall charge of the army, Churchill backed away from the window. He later wrote in *The Aftermath*, 'I remained in my room, a prey to anxiety.' After realising that they were not likely to get anybody to listen to their complaints at the War Office, the soldiers moved on to Horse Guards' Parade, where a civil servant addressed them. This was probably only a delaying tactic, because the more that the man spoke, the more angry and threatening the soldiers became. It was at this point that a troop of the Household Cavalry rode forward. At the same time, troops from the Grenadier Guards closed in from the other side of Horse Guards' Parade, with bayonets fixed and apparently ready for any eventuality. Since every one of the soldiers occupying the area was also carrying a rifle, things could have gone badly. As it was, they allowed themselves to be arrested and were then taken to Wellington Barracks. It was in nobody's interests to see a thousand court-martials held at that time and so all the men who had taken part in the disturbances at Victoria Station and in Whitehall were simply shipped off to France as planned.

This has been by no means an exhaustive account of the mutinies and strikes which took place in the British Army in 1919. By some accounts, around 100,000 soldiers took part in mutinies at one time or another during the course of that year. This mood of militancy did not end abruptly when men were demobilised from the armed forces. After having taken part in the sort of actions at which we have been looking, those who left the army were often ready to stand up to authority again in various ways. Today, we might say that they had been politicised, perhaps even radicalised. It was noticeable that during the widespread riots and disturbances which were seen across the whole of Britain in the year following the end of the First World War, soldiers and ex-soldiers were generally in the forefront of the trouble. Men wearing old army greatcoats or medal ribbons often appeared to be the ringleaders when violent protests were taking place. Indeed, associations of ex-servicemen were thought to be among the most revolutionary and dangerous elements in Britain in the years following the end of the First World War. Basil Thomson, who was Director of Intelligence in 1919, wrote of these organisations: 'In the months following the Armistice some of the societies of ex-servicemen began to give anxiety. The most dangerous at the moment seemed to be the Sailors', Soldiers' and Airmens' Union, which had whole-heartedly accepted the Soviet idea and was in touch with the police-strikers who had been dismissed, with the more revolutionary members of the Trades Councils, and with the Herald League.'

It is time now to see what the army was really needed for in Britain and why it had been so important to find out which units would obey orders and which could not be trusted. In the last week of January 1919, the situation which had been so feared by Lloyd George's Cabinet finally arrived. Troops loyal to the government were needed to put down what the Secretary of State for Scotland, Robert Munro, described as, 'a Bolshevist uprising'. Alarmingly, when it came to the crunch, it was found that the army units stationed closest to the trouble could not be relied upon. They were confined to barracks and troops from much further afield had to be drafted in. The worst fears of the British government had come true; they could not, when the time came, rely unconditionally upon British soldiers to deal with disturbances in their own country.

Chapter 4

Tanks on the Streets

Throughout the war, those labouring in the factories, mines, railways and shipyards of the United Kingdom worked extremely hard for very long hours. The nation was united in its determination to defeat the Germans. However, the final years of the war had been notable for a mood of increasing militancy among workers. It was widely acknowledged that when the fighting ended, things would need to change. There had been serious unrest in the years leading up to the outbreak of war and it was recognised on all sides that the truce between organised labour and employers was likely to come to an abrupt end as soon as the war was over. Whether, as some believed, the working classes were being infected with the spirit of Bolshevism or perhaps because they hoped that the world emerging from the greatest and bloodiest war ever known would be a better one for the average person, many ordinary workers were no longer prepared to put up with the conditions which had prevailed before 1914. They wanted shorter hours, higher pay and a greatly improved standard of living for them and their families. There was also growing anger at the number of unemployed people in Britain. The prevailing mood as the new year of 1919 dawned was best summed up as, something must be done.

In the years immediately preceding the First World War, Britain had been gripped by a large number of strikes. In 1911, the year which became known as the 'Great Unrest', 10 million days were lost to strikes in Britain. The following year, the number was 40 million. In 1914, 10 million days had been lost to strikes by the summer. The Triple Alliance of miners, railwaymen and dockers (see Chapter 5) was founded that same year and it was widely expected that the autumn of 1914 would see a railway strike, which had the potential to turn into a general strike. In a sense, the outbreak of the First World War rescued the government from a very tricky situation.

As soon as the war began, there was an enormous surge of patriotic enthusiasm and British workers in general put their disputes with employers to one side, the feeling being that everybody should muck in and do their bit for the war effort. In 1915, the first complete year of war, fewer than three million days were lost to strike action, a third of the figure for 1914. The situation was the same in 1916. After two and a half years of war, however, working men and women began to become restless again. Trouble began to reappear on the industrial front in 1917 and not only in Britain. In France, there were spontaneous strikes and demonstrations, such as those which followed the May Day parades that year. Seamstresses, bank clerks, telegraph messengers and munitions workers all withdrew their labour in the summer of 1917. A month earlier, in April 1917, 300,000 workers had gone on strike in Berlin. By that time, strikes and mutinies had already brought down the Tsar in Russia.

It is important to bear all these other events in mind, for they allow us to view what was happening in Britain in context. In 1917, the number of days lost to strikes in this country doubled. This is not the whole picture, because this figure relates only to official strikes. There were many others which were unofficial. There would probably have been a good many more strikes if the government had not, at the beginning of the war, passed a piece of legislation which had the effect of making many strikes illegal. The Defence of the Realm Act (known as DORA) was rushed through Parliament on 8 August 1914, four days after the outbreak of the First World War. It was a draconian measure, designed to give the government unlimited power to compel citizens to do some things and forbid them from doing others. One clause gave the government the power to introduce further regulations under the act, as and when they were needed, in order to 'secure public safety and the defence of the realm'. So, for instance, a regulation was added when rationing was brought in, which made it a criminal offence to feed wild animals, so wasting food. Some of the regulations brought in like this were more than a little bizarre. Regulation 40B concerned the supplying of cocaine to actresses! This Act, together with others passed after the outbreak of the war, made legitimate industrial action very difficult for British workers. For example, the Munitions of War Act of 1915 made it illegal for engineers to change their place of work without official permission and it also became an offence to criticise the conduct of the war or suggest even that the war was a bad thing in itself. A number of trade unionists fell foul of this legislation, including one who was to play a crucial role in the disturbances in Glasgow in January 1919.

In 1916, the year of the Battle of the Somme, the Clyde Workers' Committee in Scotland published a magazine called *The Worker*. This criticised the war and the police were ordered to arrest two trade unionists called Willie Gallacher and John Muir the men responsible for the article in question. They were charged under the Defence of the Realm Act and brought to court, where Muir was sent to prison for a year and Gallacher for six months. Gallacher went on to become a leading figure in industrial action in Glasgow in the years following the end of the First World War.

A year later, more workers were sent to prison following strikes in munitions factories. After the strikes spread to the Royal Arsenal at Woolwich, eight shop stewards were arrested for offences under the Defence of the Realm Act and subsequently appeared at Bow Street Magistrates' Court. It was plain to the authorities that only the fact that most workers were content to see Germany as the chief enemy and to place their own personal grievances on the back-burner until the war was over, which was preventing the unrest turning into a serious threat to the stability of the country. An enquiry into the strikes in London and other parts of South-East England, concluded that 'The unrest is real, widespread and in some directions extreme, and such as to constitute a national danger unless dealt with promptly and effectively. We are at this moment within view of a possible social upheaval or at least extensive and manifold strikes.'

There could be no doubt that as early as the year before the end of the First World War, there was the apprehension that something like an uprising by British workers might be in the air. The government was sufficiently concerned to make preliminary arrangements for arresting many more trade unionists under the Defence of the Realm Act. News of the revolution which deposed the Tsar of Russia caused unease in Britain. On May Day 1917, three months after the first Russian Revolution, a series of strikes began. The North of England was especially affected and in particular the cities of Manchester, Liverpool, Sheffield and Rochdale. Lloyd George's War Cabinet instructed Scotland Yard to draw up a list of the ringleaders, with a view to arresting them under the Defence of the Realm Act. Assistant Commissioner Basil Thomson was the man given this task, but he preferred to stay his hand and see how matters developed.

Thomson feared that mass arrests might prove to be counter-productive, provoking further strikes.

King George V was persuaded that if he and Queen Mary were to tour the North of England, that his presence might act to remind workers there of their duty. It was accordingly arranged that the King should arrive in Chester on 14 May 1917 and then spend four days touring the areas most affected by industrial unrest. It was a gamble which very nearly didn't come off, because there were genuine fears that the King's safety might not be able to be guaranteed or, at the very least, he might be heckled or insulted if he showed himself in the shipyards and factories of North-West England. Rumours about this possibility became so widespread, that Buckingham Palace was compelled to issue a press statement; assuring the public that the Royal tour would still take place. On 12 May, national newspapers carried the following press release:

> Reports have been current that the unrest in certain industrial areas had led to the abandonment of the tour which the King proposed to undertake next week. We are authorised to state that there is no truth in these reports. The full programme of the proposed tour will be carried out early next week, by which time it is believed that, as the result of recent conferences between the Government and trades unions and a fuller appreciation by workers of the nation's needs, a complete resumption of work will have taken place.

It says something about the state of Britain at this time that it had been thought necessary to issue a statement of this nature. That the King himself might have been exposed to unpleasantness in England would have been unthinkable in the opening years of the war. As it turned out, the Royal tour was only partially successful in damping down the unrest which had been growing in industrial areas. On 16 May, while the King was in Manchester, Basil Thomson wrote in his diary, 'The effect of the King's visit North has been excellent.' This was true as far as Manchester went, but strikes in Liverpool and Sheffield continued unabated. The Special Branch went ahead with its plans to arrest the men whom they saw as being behind the trouble. Lloyd George also appealed to the Trades Union Congress (TUC) for help in ending the strikes.

After the war ended with the Armistice of November 1918, a general election was held almost immediately. The Prime Minister and his colleagues correctly gauged the way that the wind was blowing and played shamelessly to the gallery when canvassing for votes. During the election campaign in December 1918, David Lloyd George had talked grandly of, 'A land fit for heroes to live in'. He had also previously mentioned, 'habitations for heroes'. Now that he had been re-elected, there were many people who were waiting to see how he was going to fulfil these election pledges. The promise of speedy demobilisation was already looking a little threadbare by the end of January 1919 and it was thought by many workers that the government might need a little encouragement if living standards really were to rise and the country was to become a welcoming place to live for all those returning soldiers and sailors, many of whom could not even find jobs.

January 1919, the period during which the government was coming to terms with the uncomfortable fact that the army was no longer to be relied upon, was also the month that industrial action reached crisis point and forced Lloyd George and his Cabinet to realise that unless a miracle were to save them, then they might very well be facing a revolution of the same kind which had overthrown the Kaiser and Tsar. The most singular and unnerving characteristic of the wave of strikes which hit two of the major cities of the United Kingdom in the first days of 1919 was that they were not led from above, by trade union leaders, but rather erupted from below and were driven by the workers themselves without reference to trade unions, employers, the government or anybody else. Like the army mutinies, these were mass actions which were taken spontaneously and wholly arranged by the men concerned. This made them exceedingly menacing to the established order. The United Kingdom of a century ago was a strictly hierarchical society, with the King and nobility at the top and various levels of authority below them, which stretched all the way down to the factory floor. Even there, there were foremen, experienced workers, apprentices and others in descending order of importance, with the boy who fetched their tea at the bottom. Everybody knew his place in such an orderly system.

When the mutinies in the army began, shortly after the Armistice, the natural instinct of senior leaders was to seek ringleaders whom they could blame for the insurrections. The soldiers had rejected the authority of their officers: this could only be because they had accepted another authority and were giving their allegiance to others. This at least was how the matter was seen by the officers trying to tackle the men who were refusing to obey orders. The idea that hundreds or even thousands of men could act as one, without anybody leading them, was too bizarre to be considered. It would have been against nature. If they were not obeying the officers, then obviously they must be obeying somebody else.

The strikes which took place chiefly in Belfast and Glasgow at the start of 1919 followed the same incomprehensible and puzzling pattern as the mutinies. The employers and even the government were quite used to dealing with trade unions and negotiating rises in wages or reductions in working hours with these recognised and official representatives of the working men. One former trade union leader, Arthur Henderson, was even a member of Lloyd George's Cabinet during the war, later becoming Home Secretary in the first Labour government in 1924. What happened in January 1919, though, was that the workers organised themselves without reference to anybody, ignored their own trade unions and presented their demands directly to the employers. They appeared to be working as a united body, with no leaders.

It had been inevitable that the end of the war would see demands for changes in working conditions in the United Kingdom. Before 1914, most skilled manual workers were putting in a 54-hour week and many unskilled labourers worked even longer hours. During the war itself, longer shifts became the norm as everybody threw his or her energy into the war effort. With Germany defeated, it was clearly understood that things would change. At the end of 1918, the TUC negotiated a reduction in hours for engineering workers from 54 a week to 47. This was not regarded as being nearly enough by most of the workers affected and when a national ballot was held, fewer than 25 per cent of the workers concerned bothered to vote. The TUC was regarded as an irrelevance and in the factories of some cities, mass meetings were held in which every man present agreed to press demands which went far beyond what the trade unions saw as reasonable. In Glasgow, for instance, either a 30- or 40-hour week was demanded, rather than the 47 hours which the TUC had accepted. Plans were laid for strike action. The main areas of militancy were Belfast and Glasgow and it was thought that if strikes there achieved their end, then the rest of the country might follow.

The object of industrial action and strikes, whatever the ostensible reasons given, are almost invariably to gain more money or shorter hours of work, sometimes both. Self-interest generally plays a large part in the process. The strikes in Glasgow and Belfast that year differed slightly, in that there was also an element of altruism involved: the strikers were fighting not only for their own ends, but also for the sake of complete strangers. This is difficult enough to understand today: a century ago it looked like utterly mad fanaticism! To that extent, the accusation made by the government that the strikes were motivated by something other than improving working conditions was quite fair.

Throughout the whole of the nineteenth century, economic and social policy in the United Kingdom was based upon the premise that individuals could be depended upon to act in their own interest. Adam Smith, the founding father of political economy, wrote in *The Wealth of Nations* that, 'It is not from the benevolence of the butcher, the brewer or the baker that we expect our dinner, but from their regard to their own interest'. In other words, these people would act in a way which best suited their own interests and this essential selfishness could be depended upon as a given. Fifty years later, one of the most famous philosophers and political economists of the Victorian Era said much the same; John Stuart Mill defining man as a being who 'inevitably does that by which he may obtain the greatest amount of necessaries, conveniences and luxuries, with the smallest quantity of labour and physical self-denial with which they can be obtained'.

According to the prevailing wisdom, the strikers in Belfast and Glasgow would have been concerned only with forcing employers to give them the most favourable working conditions and greatest amount of money which could be extracted by the threat of a strike. In fact, the demands being made ran counter to the interests of those making them and it was this which so alarmed the government in London. A poster issued by the committee demanding a general strike called for a 40-hour week. This was not because the men themselves wished for less work, but rather so that there would be more hours of work available for the greatest number of workers, including those who were currently unemployed. The poster, which urged the beginning of a general strike from Monday 27 January 1919, was headed; TO THE WORKERS; A CALL TO ARMS. It went on to say:

The JOINT COMMITTEE representing the Official and Unofficial Section of the Industrial Movement, having carefully considered the reports of the Shop Stewards and representatives of the various industries, hereby resolve to demand a 40 hours maximum working week. For all workers as an experiment with the object of absorbing the unemployed. If a 40-hour week fails to give the desired result, a more drastic reduction of hours will be demanded.

Here was a situation which went against all the prevailing theories of political economy! These workers were concerned not only for their own welfare, but also for that of men who did not even have jobs. They were prepared, if necessary, to be paid less themselves, in order that the existing hours of work should be more equitably shared around. This was a disturbing situation for the authorities for several reasons. In the first place, it was not for the workers, but rather for the government in Westminster to worry about matters such as unemployment. By agitating in this way, it appeared that a workers' council was seeking to take a hand in what should be a national policy formulated by the Prime Minister and his Cabinet. What was most frightening though was that nobody could quite believe that ordinary workers would behave in such an altruistic way of their own volition. It seemed obvious that these men were the victims of Bolshevik agitators who must be stirring up trouble and trying to incite a revolution in Britain similar to those which had taken place in Russia and were currently being suppressed in other parts of Europe. Strong action would be needed.

There were excellent reasons for the government to fear that the situation in Glasgow might descend into chaos and disorder. Shortly before the strike began there had already been serious disturbances in the city, during the course of which shooting had broken out. On Thursday 23 January, Emmanuel Shinwell, leader of the Glasgow branch of the Seafarers Union and Chairman of the Glasgow Trades and Labour Council, gave a speech at the offices of the Mercantile Marine in James Watt Street. He told a meeting of over 600 sailors of the Merchant Navy that one of the reasons that they were finding it hard to get work was because the government would not prevent Chinese workers from signing up with British ships. Later that day, two groups of sailors were waiting at the Mercantile Marine office, both sets of men hoping to be able to sign up with a ship which was about to sail. One group consisted of white sailors of the Merchant Navy, the other men were black. There were only about thirty black sailors and they were barracked and abused by the much larger crowd of white men. The gist of the dispute between them was that the black sailors were taking work away from white men who were former soldiers. In the end, the black men were chased out into the street, where a crowd gathered, which pursued them to the Glasgow Sailors' Home on the corner of James Watt Street and Broomielaw Street.

A large and angry crowd attacked the building, smashing the windows and driving the black sailors back into the street, where they fled to a lodging house at 118 Broomielaw Street. This too was besieged by the white crowd, which had by this time grown to several hundred strong. As bottles and bricks were hurled at the windows, shattering them, the black men fought back. A number of them were armed with revolvers, which they began firing down into the streets below. One white man, Duncan Cowan, received a serious bullet wound. Another, Tom Carlin, was stabbed. There were also a number of minor injuries, including a black sailor who had also been stabbed. When the police arrived on the scene in force, they recovered a pistol and ammunition.

The atmosphere around the docks was very tense later that day, with crowds gathering and threatening vengeance on foreign sailors. The next day, Shinwell gave an interview to a local newspaper, in which he blamed the previous day's riot on the hiring of black and Asian sailors. Whatever the motive for these inflammatory remarks, the result was to raise the level of tension in Glasgow to fever pitch and make the police very uneasy about any meetings which might be held in the city.

It is interesting to note that at least one of the charges made against participants in what became known as the Harbour Riot was under the Defence of the Realm Act. David Samuels, a sailor from Sierra Leone, was charged with an offence under DORA in that he had in his possession a firearm. Tom Johnson, another of the black sailors, was suspected of the attempted murder by shooting of Duncan Cowan, who had been shot in the neck and was lucky to be alive. During surgery, a bullet was extracted from his wound and handed over to the police. In the event, nobody was charged in connection with Cowan's shooting. There were similar incidents in Glasgow during the summer, which we shall deal with in a later chapter. In the meantime, we must bear in mind that there had already been one serious riot in Glasgow during the days leading up to the strike, a riot during which firearms were discharged. One of the men who would play a prominent role during what became known as the Battle of George Square, Emmanuel Shinwell, had also been heavily involved in the earlier disturbances.

At the meeting on Monday 27 January, it was resolved to press ahead with a general strike. By that time 40,000 workers were already on strike and they set about picketing those shipyards, factories and engineering works where the men were not yet striking. These men, who would today be called 'flying pickets', moved from place to place, encouraging others to come out in sympathy. It was noticed that many of the pickets were ex-servicemen, some still wearing army greatcoats or other items of uniform. Electricity supply workers came out that week and miners in Stirlingshire also stopped work. It was said that during that week, not a single trade on the Clydeside was unaffected by the strike.

On 29 January, a deputation of strikers was received by Sir James Watson Stewart, the Lord Provost of Glasgow. He was asked to order the local council in Glasgow to compel employers to grant the demands for a 40-hour week. The Lord Provost told the men that he did not have sufficient authority himself to issue such orders and that he would consult both with his colleagues and also contact the government in London. It was agreed that he would deliver an answer in 48 hours. Matters were now moving very swiftly to a climax. In Belfast, a similar strike was also taking hold, one which was threatening electricity supplies to the city. There too, it was believed that there was an underlying and subversive aim to the strike, rather than the simple and easily understood motive of more money for shorter hours.

The newspaper coverage of the crisis as Friday dawned gives an impression of just how grave the situation was thought to be. The *Manchester Guardian* told readers in its headline 'BELFAST "SOVIET"; PICKETS AS SPECIAL POLICE'. The story underneath explained how the police were welcoming the help of strikers, who wore distinctive white bands on their hats and helped to enforce order. The strike committee was deciding which organisations could be supplied with electricity and it became clear on reading the accounts that to describe the committee as a 'soviet' was no exaggeration. They were slowly taking on the functions of a governing authority. According to the reports, Glasgow was moving in the same direction as Belfast, with the electricity supply under the control of the strikers.

It must be remembered that the Spartacist Rising had only recently been suppressed in Berlin with a good deal of bloodshed. For the British government, there must have been enough similarities between what had happened in Germany and what was now taking place on the streets of Belfast and Glasgow to cause them to wonder if these strikes were intended to be the prelude to a British revolution. The Spartacist affair had begun on 7 January 1919, with the call for a general strike, precisely what the committee in Glasgow were demanding less than three weeks later. It was only the fact that the German army remained loyal to President Ebert which enabled him to put down the revolt. Had the troops refused to obey orders, then the revolutionaries might well have triumphed. That at least was the perspective from which the government in London was working. The bind in which they found themselves was that they were not at all sure that the troops nominally at their control would follow orders as readily as Ebert's had done.

Quite apart from the unrest which was afflicting the rest of Europe in 1919, the British government had their own, particular reasons for being very uneasy about the situation developing in Glasgow. In 1916, the government had been taken completely by surprise when Irish nationalists seized parts of Dublin at Easter. There was a bloody battle before the uprising was suppressed and since then, things had been slowly deteriorating until it was clear that a civil war was in the offing. There had been some stirrings of Scottish nationalism and there was no wish to be caught unawares again. Although it was not thought likely that the disturbances in Glasgow were the prelude to an armed rising of the kind seen in Dublin, the government was not inclined to take any chances. By the end of January, plans had already been made for bringing large numbers of troops and armoured vehicles into the city. Unlike the 1916 Rising, the government was determined this time to be prepared for any eventuality. If trouble did blow up, there would be overwhelming forces ready to tackle it.

From about 9:00 am on Friday 31 January, columns of strikers, led by bands and with trade union banners and red flags flying, began to arrive at George Square outside the Glasgow City Chambers. They were accompanied by a large number of unemployed workers. It was at the City Chambers, roughly equivalent to a town hall, that the leaders of the strikers were due to meet the Lord Provost and find out from him what the government's response had been. It had been agreed that they would arrive at noon, but when they did so, it was to find that Sir James Watson Stewart was in a meeting with the city's magistrates, which did not bode well. David Kirkwood and Neil Maclean MP waited patiently until the Lord Provost was able to speak to them.

Meanwhile, the crowd in George Square at the front of the Glasgow City Chambers continued to grow. It now numbered tens of thousands strong and the whole of the square was one solid mass of men. Illustration 7 shows the scene, complete with red flag and a tram which is quite unable to move. So many men were crammed into the streets, that trams were stuck, unable to continue with their journeys. Emmanuel Shinwell addressed the strikers, as did another leader, Willie Gallacher. Their speeches that morning were later said to amount to an incitement to riot. It will be recalled that Willie Gallacher had already been imprisoned less than three years earlier, for publishing material in a magazine which came very close to sedition. Shinwell of course had had been giving inflammatory speeches in Glasgow just a few days before the meeting at the City Chambers, speeches which preceded rioting and gunfire.

Lloyd George had no intention at all of negotiating with the strikers' committee: he sent word via Bonar Law, then a member of his Cabinet, that the government was not in a position to dictate hours of work to the employers of Glasgow. His main reason for declining to be drawn into the dispute was that this would undermine the official trade unions. The men in charge of the unions could be relied upon to abide by the accepted rules and Lloyd George's government wished to deal with them, rather than grass-roots committees whose aims went beyond simply economic self-interest. Later that day, Lloyd George made a public announcement, saying: 'The government is not in control of the hours of labour in shipyards, and in a reply with which I am in complete agreement, sent by Mr Bonar Law on behalf of the government to the Lord Provost of Glasgow, the reasons given which have induced the government not to interfere. The considerations which apply to Glasgow apply with equal force to the situation in Belfast.'

The Prime Minister's determination to deal only with the official trade unions, supposedly in order to avoid undermining them, needs a little explanation. It was one of the factors which ultimately prevented a revolutionary state of affairs in gaining ground in Britain that year. The trade unions, and in particular the TUC, had a strong stake in the existing British system. Some union leaders ended up as government ministers, others were elevated to the House of Lords. At the very least, it could be said that the trade unions were playing by the same rules as the government. They may have been, and on occasion certainly were, in opposition to each other, but both knew just how far they could go. The same could not be said of the leaders of the strikes in Glasgow and Belfast.

The police were out in force in and around George Square, and had orders to be on the lookout for any signs of violence or disorder. While the members of the strike committee were meeting the Lord Provost, the crowd grew increasingly restless and attempts were made to stop a number of trams and then disable them, so that they blocked the roads. Some trams were already unable to get past the protestors and this looked like a deliberate attempt to exacerbate the traffic jams which were being created. Whether this was the prelude to the building of barricades or halting all traffic in the city will probably never be known, but seeing what was happening caused the police to move into action. They began clearing a path for the trams to move past the crowds, wielding their truncheons pretty freely in the process. At the same time, mounted police appeared and began to ride at the crowds outside the City Chambers; pushing them back. The strikers retaliated by hurling bottles and stones, whereupon the purpose of the presence of the magistrates with whom the Lord Provost had been in conference became apparent. Sir James Watson Stewart, accompanied by a group of magistrates and the Sheriff Principal, emerged from the building and stood on the steps. Sheriff McKenzie then attempted to read the Riot Act. David Kirkwood, who had been one of those in the City Chambers to speak with Sir James Watson Stewart, ran out of the building when he heard the noise of the fighting and was promptly knocked to the ground by police with batons and then arrested and subsequently charged with inciting a riot. He may be seen in Illustration 8, under arrest.

The 1714 Riot Act remained in force in the United Kingdom until 1973, although it was last used in 1919. Once the Riot Act had been read out to a crowd and an hour had elapsed, then the authorities could take any actions at all that they felt to be necessary, up to and including ordering troops to open fire on crowds. The precise wording of the act had to be read by a magistrate for it to be legally effective. The words which were to be read out were as follows:

Our Sovereign Lord the King chargeth and commandeth all persons, being assembled, immediately to disperse themselves,

58

and peaceably depart to their habitations, or to their lawful business, upon the pains contained in the Act made in the first year of King George the First for preventing tumults and riotous assemblies. God save the King.

In the event, the Riot Act was not read out to the angry crowd who were fighting desperately with the police. Halfway through the reading, a thrown bottle struck the Sheriff and then somebody darted forward and snatched the paper from his hand. At the same time, somebody lunged from the crowd and landed a blow on the Chief Constable's face, cutting open his cheek. While these scenes were taking place on the steps of the City Chambers, looting began as the riot spilled over into nearby streets. Windows were smashed and more than twenty trams damaged and put out of action.

It is impossible, almost a century later, to say who started the riot. The police claimed that they had been attacked, while some of those in the crowd said that they themselves had been the object of an unprovoked assault by the police. Most probably, as is almost invariably the case when such things occur, there was blame on both sides. The government in London, however, chose to see the disorder in Glasgow as being a sinister indication that revolutionary forces were at work. Robert Munro, Secretary of State for Scotland, said bluntly, 'It is a misnomer to call the situation in Glasgow a strike – this is a Bolshevist uprising'. Again, it is difficult at this late stage to say what the strikers in Glasgow were really hoping to achieve, if anything, beyond their stated aim of a 30 or 40-hour working week. Certainly, there were communists amongst the leadership, but that does not of course mean that all the strikers were intent on overthrowing the government.

Several of the strike leaders were arrested during and after what was to become known as the Battle of George Square and charged with incitement to riot. Among them was Emmanuel Shinwell, who went on to become a Labour MP, government minister and then Baron Shinwell of Easington. By the end of the day, nineteen police officers and thirty-four strikers had been treated in hospital for injuries received in the riot. It went down in the mythology of Glaswegian left-wingers as 'The Battle of George Square' or 'Bloody Friday'.

As darkness fell on Glasgow, it became clear that the electricity supply was failing as a result of the industrial action. The lack of lighting in public places encouraged some window-breaking and a certain amount of looting, but it was nothing that the police were unable to handle. The response of Lloyd George's government to what really amounted to no more than a few broken windows and the hurling of bottles and bricks was astonishing, showing that the Cabinet was seriously concerned about what the disorder and strikes in Glasgow might mean, if left unchecked. The decision was taken to impose what amounted to martial law on Britain's second-largest city.

We saw in the last chapter that the mood of the army was uncertain and that it was by no means a foregone conclusion that troops would obey orders. This was especially likely to be so if the soldiers were being instructed to act against civilians from the same area as themselves. The revolution in Russia reached an unstoppable momentum when soldiers not only refused to fire on or even disperse crowds of strikers, but actually went over to the strikers and threw in their lot with them. During the rioting on the afternoon of 31 January, it had already been observed that men in uniform, recently-discharged soldiers, had been at the forefront of the liveliest action. There was no telling how raw young recruits might react to appeals from such older men to join them and forget their oath of allegiance. This situation, with grizzled army veterans facing police officers in street fighting, led one commentator to remark that for the first time British history, rioters were more experienced in combat than those trying to control them.

The obvious place to look for troops to use for peacekeeping duties was the barracks in Glasgow itself, at Maryhill, from where troops could quickly have been marched into position on the streets of Glasgow. However, these men were in the main Glaswegians themselves and probably had friends and relatives among the strikers. Arming such men and sending them to face the strikers would have been something of a gamble. Suppose they not only fraternised with the strikers and rioters, but deserted? It was a chance that the government did not feel inclined to take. What if the soldiers went over to the other side, with their weapons? In fact, the gates to the Maryhill Barracks were locked and the Glaswegian soldiers confined to quarters. Instead of using local forces, the War Office in London ordered 10,000 troops from other areas to converge on Glasgow and take control of the city. Some were from Highland regiments, while others were English, from Durham and Surrey. All were in full battle kit, including steel helmets and fixed bayonets. Once they arrived in the city, the troops were detailed to guard bridges, power plants, railway stations, tram depots, gas works and other strategic positions. They set up their headquarters at the City Chambers.

Journalists observing the situation in Glasgow were more than a little staggered to see just how heavily armed were the forces which arrived on the morning of Saturday 1 February, and the way in which they seemed to be prepared to fight any battle which might be needed. Machine-gun nests were established on the rooftops overlooking George Square, with Lewis guns aiming down from the General Post Office and North British Hotel. A 4.5in field howitzer was positioned outside the City Chambers. As if 10,000 soldiers backed by field artillery and machine guns was not enough to tackle any eventuality, a train arrived at about the same time that the troops were taking up their positions. This special transport was loaded with tanks and these were driven to the covered cattle market in Belgrove Street, about a mile from George Square, which was turned into a tank depot and preparations were made there, so that if things deteriorated, the tanks might be used to clear the streets. The tanks in the Belgrove Street cattle market can be seen in Illustration 9.

This massive show of force was clearly designed to warn the citizens of Glasgow that, if necessary, the government would not shrink from massacring them. If anybody in Glasgow was plotting something along the lines of the 1916 Rising in Dublin, then they would find that the army were on hand, ready to put an end to any such adventure before it had even begun. The police and soldiers worked in perfect harmony to maintain order in the city. Illustration 10 shows a joint patrol of soldiers and a police officer.

In the aftermath of the riot, the police picked up all the main leaders of the strike. Emmanuel Shinwell, David Kirkwood and Willie Gallacher were charged with 'Instigating and inciting large crowds of persons to form part of a riotous mob'. In the case of Kirkwood, the charge was absurd: he had been in the City Chambers, talking to officials, when the fighting began in the street outside. Nevertheless, a dozen of the major men in the strike were now behind bars and the strikers were left leaderless. The official unions stepped in and on behalf of the workers accepted the original offer of a 47-hour working week.

The army remained on the streets of Glasgow for a week in a massive show of force, designed to remind everybody who was really in control of the city. In Belfast, it looked increasingly as though the strike committee were the real power. They were in control of the electricity supply and decided who could and could not have it. Hospitals, for instance, could have power, although the factories could not. The *Belfast News Letter*, the oldest newspaper in Ireland, was scathing about the strike committee's talk of setting up a 'workers' Parliament'. An editorial on 4 February 1919 said, quite correctly, 'These objectives are not industrial, but revolutionary'. With the threat of Irish nationalism to contend with, nobody was under any illusions about where a separate Parliament would lead: it would mean conflict with the government in London and ultimately civil war.

By early February, electricity workers in London were planning to strike in solidarity with the men in Glasgow and Belfast, explicitly threatening to cause blackouts in London. This was enough to prompt Lloyd George to take some very tough action. In London, a number of soldiers were put on standby, with the possibility of using them to run power stations if the need arose. There was already legislation in place which would enable the government to bring a quick end to the strike there, although there had at first been some reluctance to use a law which had been specifically introduced to deal with wartime crises. However, since many people believed that the country was still at war, Lloyd George overcame his initial scruples and issued a regulation under the Defence of the Realm Act. In the case of the strike in Belfast and the threatened strike of engineers and electricians in London, a new regulation was added to DORA, which made it an offence to deprive the community of light or to encourage others to do so. Regulation 43C was brought in on 5 February and it was clearly aimed at those hoping to close down power stations in either Belfast or London:

Where a person employed by a Government Department or by a municipal authority or by any company or contractor upon whom is imposed by Act of Parliament the duty, or who have otherwise assumed the duty, of supplying any city, borough, town or place, or any part thereof, with electricity, wilfully and maliciously breaks a contract of service with that Department, authority, company or contractor, knowing or having reasonable cause to believe that a probable consequence of his so doing, either alone or in combination with others, will be do deprive the inhabitants of that city, borough, town or place, or part, wholly or to a great extent of their supply of electricity, he shall be guilty of a summary offence against these regulations. Any person guilty of an offence against this regulation is liable to six months imprisonment, with or without hard labour, or to a fine of £100, or to both such imprisonment and fine. Any person who attempts to commit or solicits or incites or endeavours to persuade another person to commit such an offence, or procures, aids or abets or does any act preparatory to the commission of such an offence, is liable to like penalties.

This was a very severe and far-ranging order, which meant that anybody making a speech in support of a strike by engineers or even writing about such a thing or talking of the possibility of industrial action in power stations could be arrested and sent to prison.

On the same day that the new regulation under DORA was published, the government let it be known that they were ready, if need be, to take even tougher action. *The Times* reported that Regulation 43C would be supplemented by 'other measures' to ensure the uninterrupted supply of electricity both to London and other British cities. Details were not given, but it was reported that: 'Conferences have taken place during the last few days at which the civil powers, the Army and the Navy were all represented, and important decisions were reached in connexion with the threatened strikes of electricians, engine drivers and others.'

It was not long before the practical consequences of these 'decisions' became clear. With government backing, the local authorities in Belfast took an increasingly hard line against the strike and eventually, by the middle of February, troops were brought in. *The Observer*, reporting on 16 February, described the scene in Belfast as the strike collapsed: 'The only important development in the labour situation yesterday was at Belfast, where the gas and electricity supplies of the city, which had been cut off for three weeks owing to the strikes, were resumed under military protection. There was no excitement. Infantry detachments were posted inside the stations at an early hour, while machine-guns commanded the entrances to the gasworks and a Lewis gun was mounted at the electricity works.'

It was now plain that if no other way could be found of ending strikes in key industries, then the army would be brought into play. This was not to be their only role in British life, however. As the year progressed, rioting and disorder on the streets was to become increasingly common and sometimes the police were unable to deal with the violence. It was for this reason that the loyalty of the army and their readiness to follow orders was of such crucial importance. The first wave of mutinies, which had so alarmed both senior officers in the army and also the government in London, appeared to being dying down by the late spring of 1919 and it was hoped that troops would be available when needed to deal with the strikes and unrest which was expected. This could crop up in the most improbable of places and the army could just as easily find themselves called in for peacekeeping duties in the Home Counties as they were in Belfast or Glasgow. This was what happened in the summer, when the Bedfordshire town of Luton became the front line in the wave of revolutionary activity which was sweeping the country that year.

Chapter 5

The Triple Alliance Flexes
its Muscles

Today, we regard the threat of a rail strike as little more than a troublesome and unwelcome inconvenience. True, it can be a very great nuisance and cause us to arrive at work late or even to be compelled to take the day off, but that is about the worst of it. After all, most of us have cars and, at a pinch, we might be able to get to our places of work by driving, instead of relying upon the train to take us there. A century ago though, strikes on the railways were regarded as precursors of civil upheaval and even the harbinger of revolution. To understand why this should have been, we need to look back at the history of railways in Britain and their use by the government.

On 24 May 1839, less than a year after the coronation of Queen Victoria, a train travelled from the port of Liverpool to Manchester, one of the great industrial centres of Northern England. This short railway journey was of great significance, not only in the story of Britain's railways, but also in military history. It was the first strategic movement of troops by rail ever to be seen in Europe. Significantly, the soldiers on board the train, men of the 10th Regiment, were being despatched not to some foreign war, but in order to suppress the disorder which was expected to follow a Chartist demonstration in the city.

Traditionally, troops dealing with riots or the threat of violence in Britain had been marched into the restive area and quartered there until things had quietened down. This meant that military forces could end up being widely dispersed and garrisons left virtually unmanned. By using troop trains, they could instead be moved quickly to deal with one outbreak of rioting and then return to their base later that same day. The railways revolutionised peacekeeping in the country and it is thought that the early adoption by the British Army of troop trains helped prevent the kind of major upheavals faced by the rest of Europe in 1848, 'The Year of Revolutions'.

In the so-called 'Great Unrest' of 1911, troops were deployed in many parts of the country, 12,500 being stationed in the capital alone. The railway system meant that whenever the need arose for soldiers to tackle rioting or take part in strike-breaking, they could be carried there in a matter of hours by train. That is, until the railways went on strike that year. Almost 60,000 troops were mobilised in an attempt to keep the railways running, but of course the system was also necessary for actually moving the soldiers from place to place. At Llanelli in South Wales, there was sabotage of a locomotive in order to block the line. Troops were first ordered to mount a bayonet charge against the crowds of strikers who were crowding round the disabled engine and then later opened fire, killing two men. That same day, strikers tampered with a truck full of dynamite which exploded, killing another four men.

With the railways out of service and trains unable to carry troops to where they were needed, it became increasingly difficult for the government in London to deal with the strike. Home Secretary Winston Churchill said bluntly, 'We cannot keep the trains running. There is nothing we can do. We are done!' In short, a smoothly-running railway network and the efficient deployment of military power went hand in hand and hindering one had an inevitable and deleterious effect upon the other. Of course, Britain was not the only European country in which this intimate relationship existed between railways and troop movements. A. J. P. Taylor famously advanced the hypothesis that it was the reliance upon railway timetables to move soldiers from one part of a country to the other which inadvertently caused the First World War to begin. Strict adherence to railway timetables meant that Germany had very little room to tinker with its plans for mobilisation and so, in a sense, was compelled to overplay its hand in 1914, with catastrophic consequences.

The railway workers of Britain had therefore, before the outbreak of war in 1914, the ability not only to paralyse the country if they wished, but also to cripple it militarily. A railway strike was viewed by some as a weapon which could be wielded not just in order to extort higher wages, but also to frustrate government actions. The industrial unrest which had plagued the country during 1910 and 1911, threatened to become even worse when the newly-formed National Union of Railwaymen (NUR), joined forces with two other unions in 1914 to present a unified front in the event of a strike. The NUR entered into an alliance with the Mining Federation of Great Britain and the National Transport Workers' Federation, which represented, among others, dockworkers, calling this arrangement the Triple Industrial Alliance. If one of the parties went on strike, the other two would, if asked, come out in sympathy. This meant, in effect, that any dispute with the railway workers, miners or dockers had the capacity, if unresolved, to escalate into a general strike which would bring the entire country to a halt.

The name chosen for what looked something like a super-union, was perhaps unfortunate. The Triple Alliance, after which it was named, was a group of three European powers with whom Britain was soon to go to war. The bloc to which Britain itself belonged, consisting of Britain, France and Russia, was called the Triple Entente. Naming an organisation after the hostile group of Germany, Austria-Hungary and Italy suggested from the start that this union of unions was likely to be opposed to the interests of the government. Certainly, it had the immediate effect of making the British government very uneasy, because with the state of industrial relations at that time, it was practically a racing certainty that either the miners, the railwaymen or the dockers would at some point strike in furtherance of a pay demand, which action could in turn trigger a general strike.

Looking at the number of days lost to strike action in the years leading up the outbreak of the First World War, we see how active the trade unions were at that time and the danger that the governments of the day supposed them to present to the country. In 1911, just over 10 million working days were lost due to strikes. The following year, the figure was 40 million. This then was the state of affairs before the First World War. In 1919, the year after the war ended, 35 million days were lost and by 1921, the total was a staggering 85 million. To put these statistics into perspective, the number of days lost to strike action at the height of the miners' strike in 1984 was just 27 million. Britain was, in the years immediately following the end of the First World War, in a far more desperate state of industrial confrontation than has ever been seen since.

In a sense, the industrial confrontations which racked Britain in 1919 were nothing more than a continuation of the strife which had been seen in the years leading up to the declaration of war in the summer of 1914. The beginning of the First World War postponed the crisis which was seen in 1919. The underlying causes of the troubles between employers and workers had not been resolved by the war and as soon as the Armistice was arranged, the struggle between the trade unions and the owners of the factories, mines and railway companies began again.

In his *War Memoirs*, published in 1938, Lloyd George said that, 'in the summer of 1914 there was every sign that the autumn would witness a series of industrial disturbances without precedent'. There was good reason for supposing that this would be the case. The country had seen unrest in many trades and industries throughout the first half of 1914. This began in January with building workers in London, carried on with threats of a general strike on the buses by the London and Provincial Union of Vehicle Workers in May and continued in July with a strike at the Royal Arsenal in Woolwich, the country's biggest arms factory. With the founding of the Triple Alliance, the stage was set for the greatest confrontation of all. There was a very real prospect that any sort of dispute in the coal mines of South Wales could escalate swiftly into a national strike of the railways. Some in the establishment chose to see this as being tantamount to treason and insurrection. The Dean of St Paul's Cathedral, William Inge, said that the leaders of the trade unions 'deserved to be executed as rebels against society'!

Although most workers threw themselves into the patriotic struggle against Germany, putting their various grievances on the back burner until the war had been won, that did not mean that there was no industrial action at all during the First World War. The discontent that had led to the serious confrontations between the army and strikers in 1911 had not evaporated. The militant trade unionists had simply decided that winning the war was a greater priority and that there would be time enough when Germany was beaten to think about challenging the established order in Britain once more.

The industrial situation in 1919 was repeatedly described by the government as being 'unprecedented'. There was good reason for this assertion. In the usual way of things, strike action is an essentially private matter, between an employer and the men and women who work for him. A stoppage or lockout might, and frequently did, become ferociously bitter, but it was still a dispute between two parties, both of which were separate and independent from the government. This position changed radically during the First World War. Because of the pivotal role played by the railways in the military preparedness of the nation, on the outbreak of war the government of Herbert Asquith nationalised the whole of

Britain's railway system. The same thing was later done with the mines, all of which had been, until that time, in private ownership. The docks too were taken under direct government control. These were all prudent and wise precautions to take when the country was engaged in the greatest war the world had ever seen.

At the beginning of 1919, the railways, mines and docks of Britain were still nationalised and under the stewardship of the government. They were state enterprises and any confrontation between workers and management was, in effect, a challenge to the state. It was this situation which made the possibility of a general strike that year such an alarming one to Lloyd George and his Cabinet. The government had been able to maintain the appearance of neutrality and stand aloof from the strikes which had brought chaos to Glasgow, but this would scarcely be possibly if the industrial action was being directed at nationalised industries.

There was of course the constant suspicion that strikes and industrial unrest in general were being fomented and stirred up by the malign influence of foreign Bolsheviks, but even without this anxiety on the part of the government, the situation would have been serious enough. A home-grown ideology which urged the overthrow of the state would be no less dangerous to the established order than some imported, ready-made belief system. A particularly worrying aspect of the matter was the way in which the strikes being carried out appeared to dovetail neatly with the unrest and open mutiny in the armed forces. If a general strike should be called, one which prevented the railways from being used to transport troops around the country, then the government would be at the mercy of the men organising such an action. Even if the soldiers could be brought by some other means to where there were strikers who needed to be dealt with, there was no guarantee that they would obey orders. Fraternisation between strikers and soldiers had been seen in the past and was a matter of great concern. The chief indication that the overthrow of the Tsar was imminent in 1917 was provided by the sight of troops refusing to disperse crowds of strikers in Moscow and Petrograd.

It was for the above reasons that Lloyd George set up an Industrial Unrest Committee at the beginning of 1919, under the chairmanship of the Home Secretary. With the threat of a transport strike in London in February 1919, this was blandly renamed the Supply and Transport Committee and was from then on chaired by Sir Eric Geddes. Geddes had, before the war, been the Deputy General Manager of the North-Eastern Railway and his experience in this field led to his being given a succession of important appointments after 1914. He was variously the head of Military Transportation on the Western Front and then later First Lord of the Admiralty. The purpose of the innocuous-sounding Supply and Transport Committee which Geddes supervised in 1919, before being given the newly-created post of Minister of Transport, was to maintain order in the United Kingdom if industrial action and subversion reached a point where the state might be unable to function normally.

The way that Sir Eric Geddes meant to maintain order in Britain, were vital services to be disrupted, was to treat it much as one would a conquered and occupied country. Britain would be divided up into sixteen administrative areas, each of which would be run by a 'District Commissioner'. This terminology was of course that used in the colonial service for those ruling subjugated territories. It is revealing that Geddes used such a title for the men who would each be controlling a large part of the United Kingdom. Food Controllers would be appointed and given draconian powers under the Defence of the Realm Act. In preparation for this state of affairs, which members of the Supply and Transport Committee regarded as more or less inevitable, a 'Citizen Guard' would be raised. These would be right-thinking men, volunteers who wished to support the authorities in their struggle against Bolshevism and subversion. Over 70,000 volunteers were recruited for this third force in 1919. Operations of the army and police would be unified and the Citizen Guard used to supplement other forces where necessary.

The unrest in Glasgow and Belfast had not yet quieted down when another crisis loomed; this time in London. Lloyd George was in Paris in February when the drivers on the London Underground began their strike. It was over a fairly trifling issue, that of whether their half-hour meal break should be included in their eight-hour day or taken separately, but it was enough to cause a walkout. In itself, the Tube strike could have been handled: there were after all plenty of buses and trams, but because some sections of the Underground had steam locomotives running on them, this looked as though it might draw the NUR into the dispute; which, through the mechanism of the Triple Industrial Alliance, had the potential to involve the miners and dockers as well. As if that was not enough, the electricity workers in London were also making menacing noises, stating that they might halt the supply of electricity to the capital.

Since this was precisely what had happened in both Glasgow and Belfast, it was anything but an empty threat. Troops were put on standby, ready if need be to take charge of the power stations.

Important as the negotiation in Paris of the final settlement to the First World War was, Lloyd George decided to return to Britain to resolve what could turn into a national crisis. Even apart from the possibility that they might be dragged into a strike by their support for the Triple Alliance, the Miners' Federation of Great Britain had grievances of their own to air. These related to wages, length of the working day and conditions of work. They had another, overtly political, demand which they were pressing, which was that the mines of Britain should be nationalised. It will be recalled that this temporary expedient had been adopted during the war, but plans were now afoot to return the coal mines to private ownership, a move which was universally opposed by those who worked in them. On his return, therefore, Lloyd George faced the threat of a general strike from two different directions. On the one hand, the miners were asking for a 30 per cent increase in wages, a six-hour working day, improvements in working conditions and the nationalisation of the mines, and on the other, the Tube strike was teetering on the brink of becoming a national rail strike. Either of these disputes had the ability to bring the agreement of the Triple Alliance into play, thus becoming a general strike, with all the consequences which that might entail for the country.

The leader of the Triple Alliance, the most important combination of unions the country had ever known, was Robert Smillie, the son of a Scottish crofter who had been born in Belfast in 1857. Although known in later life as Smillie, he was actually born Robert Smellie, a name which, perhaps unsurprisingly, he dropped as he grew older. Smillie went to live in Scotland, where he found work in a colliery, eventually becoming secretary of the Larkhall Miners Association in 1885.

By 1893, the miners of Britain were engaged in a fierce struggle to obtain what they called a 'living wage', a level of remuneration which was considerably greater than the owners of the mines were prepared to pay them. This led in the summer of that year to over a quarter of a million men going on strike. The reaction of the authorities on that occasion showed Robert Smillie, and other members of the Miners' Federation of Great Britain, just how ruthless the struggle between organised labour and the bosses could be.

As was also the case during the miners' strike of 1984 and 1985, some

71

of the worst trouble in the 1893 strike was in Yorkshire, in towns such as Barnsley and Dewsbury. Rioting at Dewsbury was dealt with by police baton charges and then, on 5 September 1893, there was more rioting in Barnsley, in the course of which a mob sacked colliery buildings. As a result of this, the Deputy Chief Constable of Yorkshire contacted the general commanding the army's Northern Division in York and requested military assistance in restoring order.

The town of Featherstone lies between Wakefield and Pontefract. There had been a lot of trouble at a mine there called the Ackton Hall Colliery and the magistrates in Barnsley felt now that troops were available, they should be brought in to tackle the fighting between striking miners and the surface workers who refused to join the strike. Windows had been smashed at the colliery, men jostled and there were fist-fights between those on strike and those who wished to work, but that was the limit of the disturbances. Calling in troops to confront the strikers was a terrible over-reaction.

The first contingent of soldiers arrived at Featherstone by railway on the evening of 7 September and consisted of twenty-nine men of the 1st Battalion of the South Staffordshire Regiment. Their arrival at the colliery was met with jeers and a few stones, but nothing more. The presence of soldiers had the opposite effect to that which had been hoped and the crowds of strikers grew increasingly wild, starting fires and continuing to hurl stones at the troops, who had been drawn up in parade-ground order and were waiting for instructions on what to do next. Eventually, a magistrate appeared on the scene and read the Riot Act. This meant that the troops could now take any necessary action to clear the area. The officer in charge insisted on being given written orders before taking any action and when this was done, he ordered his men at first to fire warning shots into the ground between them and the strikers. When this failed to have the desired effect, the order was given to fire into the crowd. Two men were killed by the volley of fire, 22-year-old James Gibbs and 25-year-old James Arthur Duggan. An hour and a half later, units of the Yorkshire Light Infantry and the York and Lancaster Regiment arrived in Featherstone, but there was no further inclination on the part of the miners for rioting.

This then was Robert Smillie's background: involvement in industrial disputes in which he had seen that the state was ready and willing to use lethal force to put down strikes. In 1908 he was elected vice president of the Miners' Federation of Great Britain and in 1915 became president of the Triple Alliance. Smillie was one of the toughest union leaders imaginable, but he was no Bolshevik revolutionary. It was this man whom Lloyd George saw as the key figure in the approaching crisis and he resolved to lay his cards on the table and speak plainly to him, cutting through the jargon and cant being used by both sides and explaining in the bluntest language what the outcome was likely to be if the Triple Alliance failed to alter its course.

In the 1930s, Smillie met with the Labour MP Aneurin Bevan, himself a former miner and after the end of the Second World War Minister of Health in Clement Atlee's administration. Smillie gave a detailed account to Bevan of the meeting to which he and the other leaders of the Triple Alliance were invited at 10 Downing Street in February 1919. He entered the official residence of the Prime Minister determined not to give an inch and to press the claims of the miners and other workers with unshakable firmness. By the time he had left, Robert Smillie and the other union leaders were in an altogether more sober and reasonable frame of mind, although they had rung no concessions from Lloyd George.

It is important to emphasise that the three men who went to tea with Lloyd George that day were not government stooges, but hard-headed and dedicated men who represented to the very best of the abilities the interests of the workers in the three industries which formed the Triple Alliance. In addition to Robert Smillie for the miners, James Henry Thomas was present on behalf of the NUR and Robert Williams for the transport workers.

It is worth pointing out that both Robert Smillie and Aneurin Bevan, who quoted Smillie's words at length, were fervent socialists with no love at all for the Liberal Prime Minister. There would be no reason for Smillie to lie to Bevan, nor for Bevan later to misrepresent what the other man had said. According to Smillie, this is what Lloyd George said to him and the other two leaders of the Triple Alliance:

> Gentlemen, you have fashioned, in the Triple Alliance of the unions represented by you, a most powerful instrument. I feel bound to tell you that in our opinion we are at your mercy. The army is disaffected and cannot be relied upon. Trouble has occurred already in a number of camps. We have just emerged from a great war and the people are eager for the reward of their sacrifices, and we are in no position to satisfy them. In these

circumstances, if you carry out your threat and strike, then you will defeat us. But if you do so, have you weighed the consequences? The strike will be in defiance of the government of the country and by its very success will precipitate a constitutional crisis of the first importance. For, if a force arises in the state which is stronger than the state itself, then it must be ready to take on the functions of the state, or withdraw and accept the authority of the state. Gentlemen, have you considered, and if you have, are you ready?

According to Robert Smillie, after hearing the case set out in this plain and unadorned fashion, he and the other two union men knew that they were beaten. Taking over the running of the country had never formed part of their plans and they had no intention at all of instigating a revolution.

Little wonder then that Andrew Bonar Law, the Chancellor of the Exchequer, remarked later that year that, 'The trade union organisation was the only thing between us and anarchy'. This, of course, was why Lloyd George did not intervene in the Glasgow strikes, lest he undermine the official trade unions. In a very real sense, the leadership of the unions were allies of the government, as anxious as the Cabinet that the political system of Britain remained intact. The unions were as much a part of the establishment as the MPs at Westminster.

This then was the nature of the revolution feared by the government of Britain at that time. It was not so much that they expected crowds of armed peasantry to storm Downing Street and Buckingham Palace, more that some development might bring into being a force which was capable of defeating the state. Once this happened, then in a sense the revolution would already have happened, without anybody needing to do anything further. The state is and must be the most powerful force in a nation; that is what it means to be the state. If that situation changes, a revolution has taken place. This was what happened twice in Russia in 1917, when the army stopped obeying first the Tsarist officers and then later that same year, the Provisional Government. This is what made the mutinies in the British armed forces so dangerous, particularly in the summer of 1919, when the police went on strike. If the trade unions showed themselves to be more powerful than the government, then a sea change must inevitably occur in the status quo.

THE TRIPLE ALLIANCE FLEXES ITS MUSCLES

Lloyd George's solution to the disputes with the miners was the simple and time-honoured expedient of setting up a Royal Commission to look into the matter. This was to be headed by Mr Justice Sankey, a High Court Judge and later Lord Chancellor in Ramsey MacDonald's administration. The Coal Industry Commission, known more generally as the Sankey Commission, was to be made up equally of businessmen and trade unionists. The setting up of this enquiry was sufficient to delay the onset of a miners' strike in February, with the consequent danger of a general strike if the railwaymen and transport workers came out in sympathy.

The speed with which the Sankey Commission set to work and produced its findings and recommendations is quite amazing when compared to modern investigations such as the Chilcot Enquiry which, six years after it was set up, still shows no sign of publishing its conclusions. The commission first met on 3 March 1919 and produced its preliminary findings just seventeen days later, surely a record for a Royal Commission! It is here that the government engaged in a little sharp practice. Bonar Law, for the government, announced in the House of Commons on 20 March that, 'I say now on behalf of the government that we are prepared to adopt the Report in the spirit as well as in the letter, and to take all the necessary steps to carry out its recommendations without delay.' This seemed to everybody, including the miners themselves, quite unequivocal.

The interim recommendations of the Sankey Commission were for a 20 per cent increase in pay and a reduction of an hour in the working day for miners. The question of nationalisation was to be the subject of the final stage of the report, which was to be published in the summer. On 23 June 1919, still less than four months after it began its deliberations, the Commission agreed that the majority of its members were in favour of some form of nationalisation: public ownership of the coal mines. There was much humming and hawing on the part of the government, and finally, almost two months later, Lloyd George made a statement about nationalisation: 'Friends and many outside seem to assume that when a Government appoints a Commission, it is in honour bound to accept all its recommendations and to put them into operation. I never heard of that doctrine in the whole history of the House of Commons.'

The Prime Minister went on to reject the idea of nationalisation of the mines, promising instead to set up a new Department of Mines, various committees and other things, such as welfare schemes for mining areas. The Royal Commission had bought him sufficient time to put the government in a much stronger position to withstand a miners' strike than they had been in February. At the height of summer, with coal stocks at their peak, it would have been little short of suicide for the miners to go on strike. There were, nevertheless, some miners who were determined to strike. In South Wales and West Yorkshire, industrial disputes closed pits for varying periods over the summer. The Royal Navy sent sailors to pump water out of the pits which were idle, so that they would still be ready for use once the strikes were settled.

There was an interesting development in the fight against the communist subversion which was supposedly rife in Britain. Basil Thomson was Assistant Commissioner and head of Scotland Yard's Criminal Investigation Department, which of course included the Special Branch, which had been set up in 1883 to combat Irish terrorism on the British mainland. For the first few years of its existence it had been called the Special Irish Branch. Originally, there had been plans to call it the Political Branch, but this was thought to sound a little too sinister and redolent of the secret police departments of many Continental countries.

During the First World War, Basil Thomson and his detectives had arrested a number of German spies, who were subsequently executed by firing squad at the Tower of London. As a result, he acquired something of a reputation for being a spy-catcher and expert in secret service work. In fact, the information which led to the capture of the enemy agents was invariably supplied by military intelligence, the department which is known today as MI5. As they had no powers of arrest, they simply passed on the names and addresses of the German agents to Scotland Yard, who arrested the men.

Thomson had a flair for self-advertisement and after the war ended, he managed to persuade members of the government that he was the man to track down Russian influence in the industrial disputes and mutinies which were becoming so prevalent. Lloyd George was impressed with Thomson and in the summer of 1919 he was both knighted and also appointed the director of an entirely new intelligence service; the New Home Intelligence Department. Sir Basil, as he now was, had a coordinating role over all the various intelligence services, including MI5 and the Special Branch. It put him in an enormously powerful position and made him the object of considerable jealousy and resentment from MI5, who regarded him as no better than an amateur.

Thomson's chief selling-point for the government was that just as he had, according to his own account, dealt with the infiltration of German agents into Britain during the First World War, so too was he now the man to tackle the Bolshevik menace which was provoking an industrial war. He believed, or purported to believe, that the Bolshevik government in Russia was behind many strikes and even that Moscow was encouraging instability in this country by telling unemployed men to claim the dole! He later wrote of this curious means of overthrowing the capitalist system in Britain. Apparently the Third International wanted those out of work to demand a rate of relief equal to the trade union rate of wages. This would bankrupt the Exchequer and bring down the country. That anybody at all could place any credence in such a bizarre scheme seems almost beyond belief, let alone that the director of Britain's intelligence service could subscribe to such nonsense. Nevertheless, Thomson later wrote that: 'These instructions were acted upon in London and other places. Most of the agitators among the unemployed were communists with headquarters at the International Socialist Club, which had received a subsidy of £1000. It is unnecessary to add that they were drawing salaries.' In other words, unemployed men who were seeking enough benefits to enable their families to survive were doing so as part of a sinister plot coordinated by Lenin in Moscow. This kind of thing made very pleasant hearing to those in power in Britain. All the unrest in the country was not, after all, the consequence of their own foolish and muddled policies; it was all the fault of the Russians. Lloyd George arranged on more than one occasion for the Director of the New Home Intelligence Department to come to Number 10 to brief MPs about the threat facing the country. According to Sir Basil, he told them: 'The routine of the "Home" section of my staff was to attend subversive meetings all over the country and to obtain evidence of money passing from Russia to the extremist section of Labour.' We shall see in a later chapter that Basil Thomson was so worried about Bolshevism that he was easily drawn into a conspiracy against the Prime Minister when it was suggested that Lloyd George was actually a traitor himself, in the pay of the Russians.

We have looked so far at the mood of the army and also at some developments in the field of industrial relations. It is time now to see what was happening on the streets of Britain's towns and cities, among the ordinary, apolitical mass of people. 1919 was remarkable not merely for the larger events which made it such a memorable year, but also for the overall attitude of the men and women who were not members of the armed forces, nor were striking. We have in recent years seen outbreaks of rioting in this country, most notably that which engulfed a number of English cities in the summer of 2011. Such riots are as nothing compared with those which swept Britain in 1919

Chapter 6

A Summer of Discontent

When PC Keith Blakelock was killed during the course of a riot in the inner London district of Tottenham in 1985, it was widely claimed that this was the first time in the twentieth century that a police officer had been murdered in this way by rioters. This was of course nonsense. The first policeman to die as a direct result of injuries received in the course of a British riot in the twentieth century had actually been killed sixty-six years earlier and had died not in some impoverished and depressed urban area, but in the pleasant Surrey town of Epsom. Sergeant Thomas Green's death on 17 June 1919 was one incident in a wave of unrest that summer, which included some of the most ferocious rioting ever to be seen on the British mainland, disorders which were eventually only quelled by the use of military force.

Before looking at the rioting which swept across Britain that year, we need to put such events in their proper context. In recent years, a myth has taken hold that civil order in this country has generally been something to take for granted and that rioting, looting and the burning-down of buildings constitutes some sort of modern malady, caused perhaps by a lack of discipline, immigration or the breakdown of traditional values in our society. Nothing could be further from the truth. In fact rioting and the beating or stabbing to death of police officers during disturbances are both as British as cricket or toasted crumpets. To give one example, in the decade following the coronation of Queen Victoria in 1838, a total of sixteen police officers were killed by rioting mobs. Such murders were so unremarkable that not all of them found their way into the newspapers. The breakdown of public order during the nineteenth century was regularly remedied by calling out the army to restore order. To that extent, the unrest which gripped the country in 1919 was not seen as being quite as shocking then as it might be today. Many people in 1919 had lived through previous episodes of civil disorder or were, at the least, aware of them.

1919: BRITAIN'S YEAR OF REVOLUTION

The rioting which took place throughout Britain in the summer of 1919 was part and parcel of the general unrest at which we have so far looked. Some was associated with the desire for soldiers to be more speedily demobilised from the armed forces, while other disturbances were connected with strike action. Then again, there were riots, such as that which saw the Bedfordshire town of Luton occupied by the army, which were merely signals of the overall dissatisfaction felt by many people, particularly former soldiers, about the state of the country. The death of Sergeant Green in Epsom, although triggered by a trivial incident of drunkenness, was really an outpouring of the rage felt at the slow pace at which colonial troops were being discharged from the army and allowed to return to their own countries. Much of the trouble involved Canadian troops and one incident led to the greatest loss of life in a riot that year.

Kinmel Camp in Wales was an army base and held 15,000 Canadian soldiers who wanted only to return home now that the war was over. They felt, with some justification, that there was no further need for their services in Britain and could not understand why they were still in this country four months after the fighting had ended. The tensions in the camp had been greatly exacerbated by the industrial unrest which affected the entire country. The strikes that year had prevented food from reaching them and there was no coal for the stoves which heated their barracks. After being on half rations for a while, due to causes which were quite beyond the ability of the officers to rectify, the anger of some of the men boiled over. The final straw came when ships which had been earmarked to carry home the Canadians were instead used by American forces, some of whom had not been in Europe nearly as long as the Canadians. By 1 March, men were refusing to obey orders. It might have been thought that this would have been a good time for the commander of the camp, Colonel Colquhoun, to stay and deal with the simmering discontent, but he had a social engagement in nearby Rhyl which he was unwilling to miss.

To understand the sequence of events, it is important to bear in mind that Kinmel was not really one camp; but rather twenty self-contained compounds, each corresponding to a military district in Canada. So there was the Quebec camp, Manitoba and so on. Some of the camps were merely designated by numbers. Outside the camp was an area known as 'Tin Town'. This consisted of various ramshackle wooden buildings, some no more than shacks, which had been set up by local entrepreneurs as shops which sold goods which the men in the camp might otherwise have found difficult to obtain. These ranged from food and soap to cigarettes and whiskey.

The trouble came to a head on the evening of 4 March, when the by now openly mutinous soldiers chose as their leader the Russian-born Sapper William Tsarevitch. Due an administrative hiccup, the men were all short of money and this was also a bone of contention. Because they could not afford to buy alcohol and cigarettes, it was decided that these would be obtained from the canteens of the officers and NCOs. Sapper Tsarevitch led a large body of men around the different camps, breaking into and looting the canteens. An alarming aspect of the rampage was that cries were heard of, 'Come on the Bolsheviks!' The red curtains in the YMCA hall were torn down and attached to billiard cues to make red flags.

After they had looted and vandalised the canteens in all but two of the compounds, the rioters turned their attention to the shops of Tin Town. Not only soldiers were involved in the looting; a number of civilians also being seen in the mobs. In all, eleven of the shops outside Kinmel Camp were looted and in some cases destroyed. Some fires were also started. Throughout the night, the looting continued, until at about midnight, an attempt was made by several hundred men to storm the Quartermaster's Stores. Officers armed with batons and sticks drove back some of the rioters, but goods were still removed from the stores. The looting and disorder finally died down at about 4:50 am on 5 March. Illustrations 11 and 12 show the aftermath of the looting of Tin Town.

At a meeting of senior officers the next day, Colonel Colquhoun was told that eleven canteens had been raided and more or less wrecked, in addition to the shops which had been looted outside the perimeter of the camp. A couple of dozen men had been arrested and were being held in the guardhouse. Although he believed that the violence had ended, Colquhoun took the sensible precaution of trying to disarm the rebellious troops. As much ammunition as possible was collected up and removed to the officers' quarters. Then the colonel ordered an immediate £2 advance on the next month's pay to be issued to the men. It was a classic case of too little, too late.

The officers' quarters and administrative centre of Kinmel Camp was based in Compound 20 and it was this sub-camp which was the focus of the trouble in the afternoon of 5 March. As the day drew on, it was clear that the men who had sacked the canteens and shops the night before were still angry and likely to create mischief. As result, the officers in Compound 20, along with some loyal troops, dug trenches around the officers' quarters, to provide a defensive perimeter. Ammunition and rifles were issued to officers and also to a detachment of cavalry who could be trusted. At 2:30 in the afternoon, the attack began and it exceeded in ferocity anything which any of those present could possibly have imagined.

The rioting which took place on the evening of 4 March was fairly chaotic and unplanned. This was not at all the case with the violence the next day. Some of the soldiers fixed cut-throat razors to broomsticks, to make improvised pikes. Others managed to obtain ammunition for their rifles and brought their loaded weapons with them when they launched their attack. Still others made a red banner, which was held between two poles. Those without weapons carried sticks and rocks. The aim of the men was apparently to take control of the officers' canteen and to seize the administrative offices of Kinmel Camp.

As the mutineers approached, the men defending Compound 20 made a sortie of their own, capturing twenty men. These were confined in the guardhouse, which was also in Compound 20. A counter-attack was launched by the disaffected troops and the guardroom was invaded, with a view to freeing the prisoners. Some of those defending the guardroom used their bayonets. Shortly after this, there was a brief gun battle between the two groups.

Gunner Jack Hickman, one of the mutineers, was shot through the heart. He also suffered several broken ribs during the hand-to-hand fighting in the guardroom. At about the same time, Private David Gillen, one of the defenders, was shot through the neck and bled to death. Another of the defenders was shot through the head and two men were killed by bayonet thrusts. One of these was Sapper Tsarevitch, viewed by many as the chief ringleader of the rioters.

Nobody was ever convicted for having a part in any of the five deaths which took place during the Kinmel Camp riot, nor for that matter for inflicting any of the bullet and bayonet wounds from which twenty men suffered as a result of the fighting on 5 March. There were fifty courts martial, resulting in sentences of imprisonment ranging from three months to ten years.

It is a matter of common observation that for whatever reason, rioting tends to occur in waves. Some years in British history have been notable for the number of riots, while others are completely peaceful. We have seen this in recent decades. The year 1981 saw rioting across much of Britain, as did 1985. Three major riots erupted in different parts of the country in 1985, all of which resulted in loss of life culminating in the death of PC Blakelock at Tottenham in October that year. More recently, there was rioting in many English cities in the summer of 2011. So it was in 1919. Riots erupted in many different cities and towns, for a variety of ostensible reasons; some incredibly trivial. These frequent disturbances added to the sense of crisis and served to make the government uneasy. When the participants were soldiers from overseas, it was possible to dismiss such disorder as being a temporary by-product of the war, which would end as soon as all those foreign and Dominion troops had returned to their own countries. This led to disorder in which the participants were soldiers being dismissed as 'military riots', the idea being that such things were aberrations, which did not reflect upon society in general. This was not possible though when, as happened in July, a town only 30 miles from London was the scene of such violence, involving only British civilians, that the army had to be called in to restore order.

The trouble at Kinmel Camp, in which a gun battle and hand-to-hand fighting ended with the deaths of five men, was very definitely a 'military riot'. Four days after the events at Kinmel, violence flared in central London. This too was later described as a 'military riot'. On the morning of Sunday, 9 March 1919, a police officer was patrolling the Strand, a major thoroughfare in London leading from Fleet Street to Trafalgar Square. He came across a group of American servicemen, some soldiers and others sailors, who were playing dice in the street. They were betting on the game, which was technically illegal. Perhaps because it was the Sabbath or possibly because there had been friction between American personnel and the police before, the officer informed the men that what they were doing was against the law and they would have to stop. Some of the gamblers were disposed to argue the point and after police reinforcements arrived, three Americans were arrested and taken to Bow Street police station.

Whatever the technicalities of the law on gaming in the street in this way, it might have been wiser for the police to turn a blind eye to the matter on this occasion, because as they tried to march their prisoners to the nearby police station, a large and menacing crowd began to gather, with the intention of freeing the men. Not only American soldiers and sailors objected to what they saw as the high-handed actions of the police. Canadian and Australian soldiers also became mixed up in the affair, as did a few English and Scots servicemen.

Although they succeeded in getting their prisoners to Bow Street, the problems for the police were only just beginning. Around 300 soldiers of various nationalities were besieging the police station and it was only with the greatest difficulty that they were persuaded to disperse. Then two more American soldiers were arrested in Aldwych and also taken to the police station. Corporal Zimmerman and Private Wilson were off-duty military policemen and the British officers suspected them of inciting the crowd. They too were taken to Bow Street, whereupon a large number of soldiers attacked the building, hurling first abuse and then stones. The police made several baton charges and more arrests. Apart from cuts and bruises on both sides, the only serious injury sustained during what the newspapers called the 'Strand Riot', was suffered by PC George Field, whose skull was fractured. A Scots soldier, James Ross Campbell, was subsequently charged with causing grievous bodily harm to the police officer.

The 'Strand Riot' and the shooting at Kinmel Camp were both borne of the same frustration which precipitated the mutinies at which we looked in Chapter 2. Soldiers who had joined up or been conscripted were angry that months after the end of the war, they were still being kept in uniform. This anger could sometimes, as at the rioting outside Bow Street police station, be expressed against any figures of authority. Among the most serious of such riots took place in June and ended with the death of a police officer.

In the Surrey town of Epsom, which is now on the edge of Greater London, there was in 1919 a convalescent camp for Canadian troops, the residents of which were recovering from illness or injury. There had already been some trouble between the soldiers and the local people. On the night of Tuesday, 17 June, some Canadian soldiers who had been drinking in The Rifleman, a public house in the High Street, began to make a nuisance of themselves by singing and indulging in horseplay. The police were called and when they arrived, they ejected the troublemakers. Out in the street, the men began to protest vociferously and one soldier in particular began swearing and offering to fight the police. After being warned about his behaviour, he was arrested and taken to the police station. Some of his comrades followed the police and their prisoner. These men began threatening the police officers and swearing at them, whereupon another man, James Connors, was also arrested for using foul language.

Up to this point, there was nothing in the least unusual about what had happened that night. The routine procedure was that the police would hold the men overnight in the cells and then in the morning, when they had sobered up, the prisoners would be handed over to the military police at the base. Inspector Pawley though, who was in charge of Epsom Police Station, felt a little uneasy. He kept more men on night duty than was usually the case. His fears proved to be justified, because an hour or so later, the police officers in the station heard the sound of bugles coming from the direction of the Woodcote Park convalescent camp, together with a lot of shouting. The Inspector at once telephoned neighbouring police stations to call for urgent assistance. Word was also sent to local officers to come at once to the station, as Inspector Pawley thought that there was the chance of a drunken mob attacking it.

Despite all the precautions which he had taken, the Inspector had gravely underestimated the peril which he and his men faced. It was later estimated that a body of 400 soldiers arrived at Epsom police station, determined to free the two men who had been arrested earlier that evening. Shortly before the riotous mob of Canadian soldiers arrived, Sergeant Thomas Green had cycled to the station. Green was fifty-one years of age and had been in the force for twenty-four years. Although he was off duty, upon hearing the shouting and bugles, he had put on his uniform and hurried to the police station, in case he could be of any help. Illustration 13 is of Sergeant Green, shortly before his death.

In addition to Inspector Pawley, there were now twenty-three other police officers in Epsom police station. Although Pawley and his men were not looking for a confrontation, they obviously could not surrender to an angry mob and so prepared to defend the building. The men outside were determined not to leave without their fellow soldiers and soon began uprooting the iron railings which surrounded the police station and also digging up and breaking the paving stones which made up the path leading to the front door. Using the broken paving stones as ammunition, the infuriated Canadians proceeded to smash every window and then pressed forward with the evident intention of storming the place.

It proved fairly easy for the soldiers to break down the doors of the police station and force their way into the building, but Inspector Pawley was ready for them and led all his men in a sudden charge, beating back the attackers with their truncheons. It was in the course of this melee that Sergeant Green was struck on the head with one of the iron railings and killed. It was later said that the inside of the police station resembled a slaughterhouse, with blood splashed liberally up the walls. Inspector Pawley, four sergeants and eight constables were seriously injured, but they had also managed to inflict some severe wounds on the attackers.

After the soldiers were driven out of the police station, they made attempts to set fire to the building, but eventually they returned to the camp. After the fighting had ended, reinforcements arrived from as far away as Wimbledon and Wandsworth in South London. Over 100 police officers arrived, all on bicycles. Together, they managed to secure the police station and prepared to defend it against further attacks, although the rest of the night was peaceful. Illustration 14 shows the police station the following morning, being guarded by police officers and soldiers.

This was the first time in twentieth-century Britain that a policeman was killed in the course of a riot, although such deaths had been far from uncommon during the Victorian Era. To add insult to injury, the mob had managed to get to the cells and free one of the men who were being detained for drunkenness. The murder of a police officer on duty caused something of an uproar in Epsom, as well it might, and the news was carried in the national newspapers as well. A number of Canadians were arrested and seven were charged with rioting and manslaughter. At the inquest into the death of Sergeant Green, the coroner announced that if the person who had actually struck the blow which killed the policeman could be identified, then that man would be guilty of wilful murder. As it was, the case was treated as being manslaughter by the members of the mob whom witnesses placed at the scene.

The aftermath of the first case for some years of a policeman being killed by a crowd was something of an anti-climax. Two of the seven men who appeared at the assizes a few months later were acquitted of all charges and the remaining five convicted only of riot. They were sentenced to a year's imprisonment, but in December 1919 were granted a Royal Pardon and swiftly deported to Canada, which was what they had wanted all along.

There was a subscription for Sergeant Green's widow and the men who defended the police station were awarded gold watches for their valour. The gravestone of the man murdered that night bears the following inscription:

A SUMMER OF DISCONTENT

In memory of SPS Thomas Green who found death in the path of duty.
He was killed in defending the Epsom Police Station against a riotous mob.

Ten years later, there was a curious postscript to the death of Sergeant Green. In 1929, when most people had forgotten all about it, one of the men who had been tried in connection with Green's death went voluntarily to the police in the Canadian city of Winnipeg, where he was living. Allan McMaster, who was by then thirty-nine years old, had been one of the men convicted of riot, but acquitted of manslaughter at the Guildford Assizes ten years earlier. His conscience had been troubling him and he now wished to confess to murdering the policeman. When the Canadian police contacted Scotland Yard with this news, there was consternation. Nobody had the least desire to rake up the matter at that stage and so they simply replied that the incident had already been dealt with by the courts and that they had no interest in reopening the case. McMaster was released and that really was the end of the whole business.

It was possible to treat rioting, and even murder, carried out by troops for other countries as being of no great significance to Britain. These people were, after all, foreign soldiers and their actions cast no light on the feelings and wishes of ordinary men and women in this country. Once they were sent back to America, Canada or Australia, then things could return to normal. That this attitude on the part of the British government was mere wishful thinking is illustrated by what happened in the quiet town of Luton in Bedfordshire, just a month after the murder of Sergeant Green in Epsom. On this occasion, there were to be no foreign or Dominion troops to blame: the whole series of events was purely a product of the social tensions which were reaching breaking point throughout much of Britain that year.

It was probably hoped that the mutinies which had plagued the British Army in the months following the Armistice would cease to be a problem once the soldiers taking part had been demobilised. In a sense, this was true, but once they had been discharged back into civilian life, the rebellious feelings which had prompted the mutinies did not simply vanish. Instead, they were channelled into new directions, chief of which was a dissatisfaction with the state of post-war society. For many of those released from the army, there were no jobs to go to and this created a lot of ill-feeling towards those individuals higher up the social scale, men who seemed to have done well out of the war such as businessmen, speculators and politicians who had not even fought in the war, but still apparently thought that they were in some sense superior to ordinary, working-class men and women. This casual assumption, that despite the tremendous sacrifices made by so many families the social system would remain essentially unchanged in the coming years, infuriated the unemployed men who felt that now that they had served their purpose they had been abandoned. Just as politicians and the writers of newspaper editorials had predicted, the 'Masterless Men' were once more prowling the streets of Britain.

This situation, with unemployed ex-soldiers thronging the streets, was of course precisely what Lloyd George and his government had hoped to avoid. It was one of the reasons that demobilisation had been proceeding at a snail's pace. Those in authority might have thought that now more and more men were being sent back to civilian life, they would at least be grateful for their demobilisation orders, which only goes to show how even very clever men like Lloyd George could be stupendously wrong.

It did not take much to trigger rioting in 1919. Even soldiers who had been demobilised from the army were prone to violent behaviour if they felt themselves wronged. On 26 May, for instance, the Federation of Discharged and Demobilised Soldiers and Sailors held a rally in Hyde Park, which was attended by over 10,000 ex-servicemen. The complaint was that former soldiers were finding it impossible to get work. After the meeting, the men made their way to Parliament to make their feelings known. When the police blocked their way, a riot erupted, with bricks and bottles being hurled at them. Mounted police charged the demonstrators, driving them away from the Houses of Parliament.

Although the Armistice had been signed in November 1918, the treaty which brought the First World War officially to a close was not signed until 28 June the following year. It was decided to celebrate the event with a 'Peace Day', which was to be 19 July 1919. On that Saturday, there would be parades and festivities across the whole of Britain, including the unveiling of the new Cenotaph in London. This was only a preliminary, plaster-and-wood version of the stone structure which we know today. Although London was of course to be the focal point of the celebrations, many other towns decided to mark the occasion with fireworks, banquets and processions. One such town was Luton, which is about 30 miles north of London.

Luton Town Council enthusiastically embraced the idea of marking the end of the war and the signing of the peace treaty at Versailles with a conspicuous series of displays. There were to be floats, brass bands and a grand procession through the town, all leading up to a spectacular firework display in the evening. The Mayor and town councillors spared no expense to celebrate Peace Day. It was, after all, not their money they were spending, but that of the town's ratepayers. There was also to be a Mayoral banquet, to which Mayor Henry Impey invited councillors and various personal friends. Not a single ex-serviceman was invited to attend. This was especially galling, because neither the Mayor nor a single member of the council in Luton had actually served in the armed forces. All had belonged to what were known as 'reserved occupations', jobs which were thought to be too important for a man to be conscripted into the army. Some of the councillors had been running the Luton Corporation Food Control Committee and there was a lot of resentment towards them because it was thought that they had been profiteering from food shortages. They were, in short, the types that future Prime Minister Stanley Baldwin described as, 'Hard faced men who looked as though they had done very well out of the war'. That such men should be indulging in a 'banquet' at a time of great hardship for many families who had lost relatives in the fighting, was thought to be in bad taste.

As a mark of their disgust at the proposed 'Mayor's Banquet', one of the organisations for former servicemen tried to arrange an alternative event on Peace Day. The Discharged Sailors and Soldiers Association applied to the council for permission to hold a religious service on the same day as the official events on 19 July. They wished to use Wardown Park, a local recreation ground, for this, but the request was turned down by the Tolls and Municipal Buildings Committee. As Peace Day dawned, there was therefore a great feeling of resentment among ex-soldiers and their families against Luton's Mayor and council. It was decided to stage a rival march to the official procession and the aim was that this should arrive at the Town Hall at the same time as that organised by the Mayor.

The floats and bands of Luton's celebratory parade reached the steps of the Town Hall at the same moment that a large group of demobilised soldiers also turned up. At the front of this unofficial party were maimed and disabled former servicemen and it was obvious from the beginning that the overall sympathy of the crowds of onlookers was with the soldiers, rather than the dignitaries of the council. When the Mayor appeared on the steps of the Town Hall, resplendent in his robes of office and with a gold chain around his neck, there were calls for him to explain the decision to deny the discharged servicemen the use of the park for their service. These were ignored and when jeering and angry shouts began, the police advised the Mayor to retreat into the Town Hall.

It was by now becoming apparent that the festivities would not be proceeding according to plan. Police officers locked the doors to the Town Hall, but a number of men broke them down and led an angry mob into the building, where they smashed up furniture and then threw it out of the windows. Another group went onto the balcony and ripped down the bunting and electric lamps which had been strung across the front of the Town Hall. While this was going on, a crippled ex-soldier made a speech from the steps, calling for increased assistance for disabled and unemployed ex-soldiers. The police made frantic attempts to summon reinforcements, eventually reaching the Chief Constable, who drove to the Town Hall and succeeded for a while in calming things down. Some of the crowd moved off to the Mayor's home, to see if he would be available to answer their questions there. In fact, Henry Impey was hiding in the Town Hall, having been advised by the police that it would not be safe for him to show himself on the streets of Luton that day. As darkness fell, things grew much uglier.

The celebrations of Peace Day had been abandoned and the only question in the mind of the police was whether they would be able to contain the situation in the town overnight. There were still many people milling about on the streets and their mood did not look cheerful. Telephone calls to London for more officers to be sent were met with the response that no men could be spared for what it was assumed was only a minor disturbance in a quiet town.

At ten that evening, a new body of men approached the Town Hall. These had come equipped with hammers, crowbars and half-bricks. It was at once clear that these men were intent upon causing damage. The police spotted soldiers in uniform among the civilians. At a prearranged signal, bricks and stones were hurled at the windows of the Town Hall and nearby Food Office, smashing the windows. Then, men began making

1. The *Queen Elizabeth* class battleship HMS *Valiant*. In the summer of 1919 she was moored off Liverpool as a show of force.

2. A soldier and a Medium Mark C Hornet tank in the centre of Liverpool during the riots of August 1919.

LAWLESSNESS AT LIVERPOOL.

TROOPS FIRE OVER PILLAGING CROWDS.

RENEWAL OF DISORDER LAST NIGHT.

WARSHIPS DESPATCHED: TANKS ARRIVE.

3. A headline from the *Manchester Guardian* about the disorder in Liverpool.

5. Prime Minister David Lloyd George.

4. General, later Field Marshal, Sir Henry Wilson, Chief of the Imperial General Staff in 1919.

6. Secretary of State for War Winston Churchill.

7. The Red Flag is raised in Glasgow on 31 January 1919, shortly before troops were sent in.

8. The arrest of David Kirkwood after the 'Battle of George Square' in Glasgow.

9. Glasgow's indoor cattle market being used as a tank depot following the rioting in the city.

10. Troops and police on duty together in Glasgow.

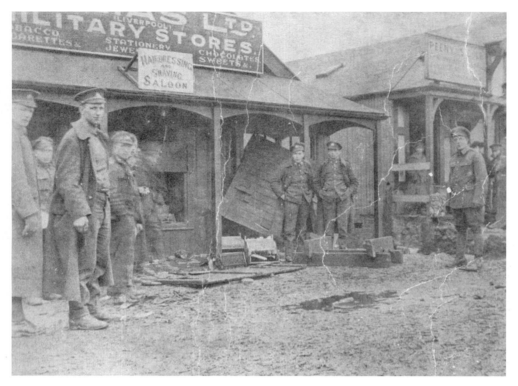

11. Damage to shops near Kinmel Camp near Rhyl in Wales after the rioting and gun battle there on 4–5 March 1919.

12. The aftermath of the rioting at Kinmel Camp, which cost five lives.

13. Sergeant Thomas Green, who died at Epsom Police Station on 17 June 1919, the first police officer to be killed in a riot in twentieth-century Britain.

14. A soldier and police officer on guard outside Epsom Police station after the murder of Sergeant Green.

15. A painting by an eyewitness of Luton Town Hall in flames during the riots of 19 July 1919. *(By kind permission of Wardown Park Museum)*

16. The burnt-out shell of Luton Town Hall after the riots.

17. Boarded-up shops in Coventry, after the rioting there in the summer of 1919.

18. Police officers on strike in London in 1919.

19. A soldier guards a looted shop in Liverpool.

20. Tanks on the streets of a British city in 1919: an unprecedented event that has been all but forgotten today.

concerted effort to get into the Town Hall again. The police made several baton charges to try and drive them off. In the midst of all this, Henry Impey, the wretched Mayor whose extravagance had triggered the riot, was smuggled out of the Town Hall disguised as a special constable. There was a very real fear on the part of the police that if Impey fell into the hands of the rioters, then they might lynch him.

As fast as the vastly-outnumbered police beat off one assault on the Town Hall, another was made elsewhere. Burning material was lobbed through the broken windows and the officers rushed from place to place, frantically extinguishing the small fires. They might have saved the building if the rioters had not broken into a garage and begun looting it for cans of petrol. Once this was poured through the windows of the Town Hall and set on fire, there was little hope that the police could cope with the resulting blaze. The fire brigade arrived and found their vehicle attacked and the hoses slashed. By the time that the brigade managed to get one hose working, it was too late to save the Town Hall and adjacent Food Office. Working with the police, the hose was used to try and clear the streets of rioters, rather in the manner of a water cannon. A painting of the Town Hall burning, painted by an eyewitness, is seen in Illustration 15. This image is eerily reminiscent of news photos of the 2011 riots in England, yet it dates from almost a century ago.

Other shops in the centre of Luton were looted, including one selling pianos. Two grand pianos were manhandled into the street and an impromptu street party held by the light of the blazing Town Hall. So many police officers had been injured by this time that the Chief Constable felt that he had no choice but to appeal for military assistance. At 3:00 am a body of troops from Biscot Camp marched into the town. These men, from the Royal Field Artillery, formed a cordon around the Town Hall and the other burning buildings, as well as the looted shops. At dawn, a large contingent of troops from Bedford drove into Luton. These steel-helmeted soldiers with fixed bayonets occupied the centre of Luton for the next week. Illustration 16 shows the burned-out remains of Luton Town Hall. Trouble flared again after dark on Sunday, but as the *Manchester Guardian* reported on 22 July: 'There were renewed disturbances on Sunday evening, but the effect of the military occupation of a number of places in the town has materially helped to subdue the riotous tendencies which resulted in so much damage being done on Saturday.'

The rioting in Luton and need for the use of troops to control the situation was a shocking reminder to the government of how close the country was to anarchy and disorder. It would have been bad enough if the events in Luton had been an isolated and atypical incident, but they were not. What was most frightening about the disorder that summer was that it took place not in the slums of Glasgow or Liverpool, but in perfectly ordinary little towns in the south of England. Take Swindon, in Wiltshire, for instance. After they had staged their own Peace Day celebrations on the Saturday, a commemorative flagstaff was erected outside Swindon Town Hall. This was a very expensive enterprise and there were murmurs in the town that the money could have been better spent on alleviating poverty among the families of men who had died fighting during the war. On Monday 21 July, the flagstaff was burned down in protest. The crowds responsible for the arson then moved on to the police station and besieged it. Windows were broken and looting of nearby shops began. The police responded with a baton charge, in which one member of the crowd suffered a broken leg.

Of course, we view today the calling out of the military to subdue unrest as being a thoroughly shocking development, but in 1919 such a move was regarded more phlegmatically. Even during the war, disorder and violence had been simmering away just below the surface of British society and the government were under no illusions at all about how any outbreak of rioting would need to be dealt with. In the summer of 1918, industrial action had halted the buses and trams of London for some days. This was caused by women demanding equal pay for doing the same work as men. The following month, there was a short strike on the Great Western Railway, which had the effect of closing down Paddington Station. At the same time, there were reports that workers in the East End of London were growing dissatisfied with both their conditions of work and also the unavailability of certain foodstuffs. The reaction of Lloyd George's government to all this was direct and unequivocal. A company of the Scots Guards was despatched to the East London district of Stratford, to be on hand if any trouble should erupt, troops with fixed bayonets being the obvious way to tackle mutinous or discontented workers.

In the space of a little over a month, the quiet towns of Epsom, Luton and Swindon had been the scene of ferocious riots, which left one police officer dead and many injured. There had been looting and arson, which had resulted in one case in the army being brought in. The Midlands too had seen serious disorder at the same time. In June, rioting had broken out in Wolverhampton following the arrest of a demobilised soldier. Crowds assembled outside both the Town Hall and police station, hurling stones and breaking windows in the buildings. The fire brigade were called out and used their hoses to drive the rioters back. Police then made a number of baton charges.

At Bilston, a town near Wolverhampton, trouble started during Peace Day, with the arrest of two soldiers. An angry mob, made up of over 2,000 people, surrounded the police station where the men had been taken and demanded their release. When the police refused, the crowd began breaking down a brick wall and using it for ammunition. After smashing the windows, petrol was poured in and lit. Fortunately, there were enough officers in the building to deal with the fires. Reinforcements were summoned by telephone and the streets eventually cleared. On the Sunday following Peace Day, shop windows were broken in Coventry and looting began. This was repeated the next day and spread to Birmingham. Once again, baton charges were used to disperse the mobs. Looted shops in Coventry, their fronts boarded up, may be seen in Illustration 17.

The riots at which we have looked in this chapter had a number of similarities. In the first place, they followed the same pattern of smashing windows and attacking the police. The arrest of soldiers, either serving or recently demobilised was a common factor in several of the cases. All the riots involved more than a handful of drunks or young hotheads. These were no ordinary Saturday-night disturbances of the kind one might see after the pubs closed. There were serious attempts to destroy civic buildings and police stations, and also to harm police officers and firefighters.

It was difficult for the government accurately to gauge the seriousness of the threat which these sporadic riots posed. It must be remembered that throughout the whole of the nineteenth century, rioting had been something of a *leitmotif* of British society, with violent disorders taking place for the most trifling reasons. Such disturbances had ranged from crowds surging through the streets after the pubs had closed to organised insurrection and rebellion against local property owners and magistrates. Some minor flare-ups resulting from an arrest for drunkenness might end with the death of a police officer and larger-scale disturbances might require the reading of the Riot Act and the use of the army. In 1919, the memories of such things was fresh and it was thought by some politicians that the disorders which they faced were no different from those which had intermittently disrupted life in Victorian Britain.

In themselves, the street violence and attacks on police stations which took place in 1919 might have been seen as being of no great significance. It was the fact that they were taking place against a background of industrial unrest, mutiny in the armed forces and talk of revolution which made them so alarming to those in authority. Rumours were rife throughout the country that army units were refusing to obey orders and that they would not take any action against working people. Such stories had been circulating since the last year of the war and had become widely believed. There was almost certainly some truth in them. We saw that in Glasgow in January 1919, it was felt prudent to use troops from outside the city to deal with the crowds of strikers, lest Glaswegian soldiers might feel a dangerous affinity for the men whom they could be called upon to face.

Legends such as these do not emerge from a vacuum and the idea that soldiers would have to be brought from outside a working-class district if they were to be expected to confront strikers or rioters was around a year before the army were called in to patrol Glasgow. We saw that when trouble was expected in the East End, in the summer of 1918, it was the Scots Guards who were brought in to be ready to deal with it. Even before that, in January 1918, it was widely believed that local army units could not be relied upon to put down any rebellion in their home towns. That these rumours were very widespread may be seen by the fact that they even reached the ears of an upper middle-class literary figure like Virginia Woolf. Writing early in 1918, she claimed to have heard of 'food riots & strikes at Woolwich & the guards have notice to march there at any moment & fire on the people, which their own Woolwich regiments would refuse to do'. The idea of army units being disaffected and unwilling to act against members of their own class was current well before the crucial year of 1919.

It is customary to draw a distinction between common-or-garden brawling of this sort between opposing groups of workers and the overtly political actions of those who seek to overthrow the authority of the state in a revolution, but the two types of disorder are often indistinguishable to the observer. The outbreaks of shooting which took place in the docks of Britain in the summer of 1919 look very similar to the events which were taking place in the rest of Europe at that time, when shooting began

94

for various reasons. Rioting frequently takes place in waves across a country, although the ostensible reasons for each individual disturbance may be very different. Sometimes it is associated with industrial action, on other occasions, race plays a part and then again there are outbreaks of disorder which appear to be altogether opportunistic and criminal in nature. What most such events have in common is an overall opposition to authority and a desire by the lowly and dispossessed to hit out at those whom they believe to be responsible for keeping them in their condition, whether these are their social superiors, men who are seemingly depriving them of jobs or simply the police officers and soldiers who wish to clear them from the streets.

The summer of 1919 was a hot one, which always increases the risk of rioting and disorder. People are far readier to smash windows, throw bricks at the police and even open fire with pistols on hot, sunny days, than when it is cold or raining. The state of Britain was such that even trivial disputes seemed to trigger major problems for public order.

Although there have always been small numbers of black and Asian people living in this country, especially in ports such as London, Liverpool and Cardiff, the First World War brought an influx of black sailors and former servicemen from places such as India and the Caribbean to Britain. With competition stiff for available jobs, anything or anybody which seemed likely to jeopardise a man's chance of finding work was a matter of great concern. It is possible that some ships were actually giving preference to black seamen, who were prepared to work for lower wages than many British sailors. This was one motive for resentment. It should be pointed out that in other cases, there were ships which refused to engage black seamen, on the grounds that white men would not live and work with them. The other perennial cause of friction between black and white people in Britain was the belief that black men had a fixed and undesirable interest in white girls. As in the United States, this ancient myth caused a great deal of mischief. Many of the race riots which took place in 1919 were precipitated by the sight of black men in the company of white women.

On Wednesday 4 June 1919, a scuffle between a black dockworker and a white man in Liverpool escalated into a riot, in which blacks and whites fought each other in the streets with knives, razors and revolvers. The *casus belli* could scarcely have been more trivial: a black man in a public house was asked for a cigarette and assaulted when he refused.

The following day, he and some friends returned to the pub, seeking revenge. What began as a fistfight soon spilled out onto the street and escalated into the use of razors and knives. A policeman who tried to intervene was knocked unconscious. Police reinforcements arrived and the black sailors retreated into a lodging house. Things then became extremely serious.

As the police approached the house where the black sailors were, a crowd of white men gathered, expressing their anger against the black sailors in the house. It was at this point that shooting erupted, with the men in the house firing down at the police as they tried to gain access. Police Sergeant Getty was shot in the neck. Another officer, Constable Brown, received a bullet wound to his mouth. The gunfire infuriated the crowd and when one of the black men, 24-year-old ship's fireman Charles Wooten, ran from the lodging house in an attempt to escape, the police quickly caught him. A rumour went around the crowd of white men, which now numbered several hundred, that the man the police had detained was one of those who had been firing at them. Wooten was wrestled away from the two police officers who had hold of him and thrown into the harbour where, unable to swim, he drowned. This was the first of a number of deaths resulting from the rioting in British ports that summer.

Thirteen black workers were arrested by the police after the riot and charged with riotous conduct and the attempted murder of three police officers The fact that firearms were being freely used against the police elevates a riot of this kind into a different category from the run-of-the-mill sort of scuffling and roughhousing which was a regular feature of life in the Liverpool docks. Over the course of the next week, things deteriorated and newspaper reporters filed stories about thousands of excited people congregating in the streets and waiting for the trouble to begin. Black people who appeared in the streets were chased and assaulted and a number of houses where black sailors were staying were looted and set on fire.

It is instructive to compare the sequence of events in Liverpool with those in Glasgow six months earlier. In Glasgow, the race riots preceded the main rioting which led to the armed forces being brought in. They acted perhaps as a catalyst, setting the stage for the main show. So too in Liverpool, where the rioting between blacks and whites in June was a curtain-raiser to the dreadful events during the police strike which ended with warships and tanks being despatched to the city to maintain order.

A SUMMER OF DISCONTENT

In London, the rioting against black people, Chinese, Arabs and people from South Asia began a little earlier. There too, firearms were involved. On 16 April, *The Times* reported that: 'Last night there was a serious riot in the East End, arising out of a feud which has existed for some time between white and coloured seamen arriving at the Port of London. Trouble occurred in a number of cafes in Cable Street, near Leman Street. About half past nine o'clock the neighbourhood was startled by the noise of firearms and the breaking of glass, and in a few minutes a crowd of men were engaged in a violent fight in Cable Street.' As was commonly the case, the trouble began when some white men objected to white girls consorting with non-whites, in this case Arabs. It is unclear from subsequent reports just who was shooting at whom, but there is no doubt that revolvers were fired during the disturbance. Knives were freely used as well and three days later a black man called Nathaniel Cassan appeared in court and was sent to prison for six months for stabbing a white man. Some of the other sentences received by participants in the riot strike us today as astonishingly lenient. Mahomed Ahmed, an Arab seaman was fined just £2 for discharging a revolver during the riot!

A month after the Cable Street riot, there were four days of rioting in the East End, which was also between black sailors and white mobs. Once again, firearms were used. Reporters estimated the crowds of white men besieging local lodging houses which contained black seamen as numbering between 4,000 and 5,000 strong. On 27 May, at the height of the disorders, a Jamaican sailor called John Martin fired a pistol at the crowd surrounding the house where he was staying. He wounded a 27-year-old white man called James Hanrahan. On that same day, another black seaman called Charles Smith was spotted with a revolver in the Commercial Road. When challenged by the police, he threatened to open fire.

There was more fighting and minor rioting in London in June and then in August, shooting broke out again in the East End, when a white crowd pursued some black seaman. The sailors drew revolvers and began firing over the heads of the mob to discourage them. When the police arrived, they arrested the three men who had been shooting in the street. The magistrates took, once again, a very lenient view of the discharging of guns in the street. They were merely fined £1 each for possessing revolvers without a licence.

The worst of the racial violence during the summer of 1919 took place in South Wales, of which Cardiff was the epicentre. In May, there had been fighting between black and American sailors. A number of shots had been fired and three black men charged with attempted murder and shooting with intent to maim. It will be noticed that the use of firearms, invariably revolvers, was the exclusive province of the black men who were caught up in the rioting. It is probable that some men at that time, fearing that they might be the victims of white mobs, had taken the precaution of arming themselves so that they could frighten off attackers. Some of the crowds which were chasing and assaulting black men consisted of thousands of angry members. The consequences for anybody caught by such mobs could be fatal, as in the case of Charles Wooten.

The main rioting in Cardiff began on 11 June and was caused by a number of white men seeing a party of black seamen accompanied by white girls. Words were exchanged, which became heated. In no time at all, the whites were throwing bottles and stones to which the black men responded by firing pistols. The police, who were quickly on the scene, were unable to cope with the situation and more shooting broke out. One black man was knifed. A very large crowd of white men gathered and moved into that part of Cardiff which was known locally as 'Nigger Town'. This was where most of the black people in the city lived. Houses were attacked and the occupants retaliated by firing at the crowd. Several homes were broken into and one house was set on fire.

Not surprisingly, the police were far from pleased to find that guns were being freely used on the streets of their city. Because of the other factors at which we have already looked in this book, things were tense enough without the sound of shooting echoing through the streets. They arrested all those upon whom they could lay their hands who had been handling or firing guns during the rioting. Mohamed Ali was found guilty that summer of shooting at the police in Cardiff and so was Mohamed Khalid, who was convicted of firing at the police with intent to murder. Then, as now, the police found themselves playing piggy in the middle when disorder between two groups of angry men began and much of the shooting, both in Cardiff and other cities, was at them.

The situation in Cardiff during June was now spiralling out of control and it was felt in some quarters that the time was fast approaching when troops would need to be brought in to restore order. On 11 June, a young discharged soldier called Harold Smart went up to a police officer in the street and said that his throat had just been cut by a black man. So it proved, because despite his being rushed to hospital in a taxi, Smart bled to death. Nobody was ever arrested in connection with this death. Another fatality in the riots was an Irishman called John Donovan, who was shot dead. The circumstances of his death showed that he was not exactly an innocent man. He had been part of a mob which was surrounding a house which contained eleven black men. The white crowd stormed the house and set it on fire with the men still inside. It was this which caused the trapped men to try and drive back the attackers by firing at them and Donovan fell at once with a bullet through his heart.

The police initially arrested all those who had been in the house which was attacked by the crowd which included John Donovan. They subsequently released all but two of the men. These were charged with murder. When they appeared the following month at the Gloucester Assizes, the jury took a robust and common-sense approach to the case. The two men in the dock were charged both with the murder of John Donovan and also with discharging firearms at persons unknown. They were acquitted of both offences, the jury deciding that they had only been acting in self-defence.

It was not only the threatened black and Arab seamen who were using firearms during the rioting in Cardiff over the course of those three days in June. Some of the reporters present in the city claimed that the white crowds were being led by what were described as 'colonial soldiers'. These were Australians who had not yet been demobilised. Some were in uniform and carrying rifles. One observer said that 'The methods adopted by the soldiers were those of active service, and the men, after firing from the prone position upon the blacks, crawled back to safety.' In other words, gun battles were erupting in Cardiff. Under the circumstances, it is a wonder that more people were not killed or injured. In fact it was widely suspected that those injured by gunfire avoided going to hospital to have their wounds treated, lest they came to the attention of the police as a result.

The number of people killed during the three days of rioting in Cardiff that June will probably never be known for sure. Some of the deaths might not have been connected with the rioting, but were perhaps just common-or-garden murders of the sort which take place from time to time in any large city. For example, the body of an unidentified black man was found one night during the riots. He had been stabbed to death. The circumstances surrounding the death of another black man showed that it was definitely a direct consequence of the disorder which was racking the city during those three days in June.

On 12 June, a crowd gathered outside 264 Bute Street, a house exclusively occupied by black men, mostly seamen. The police arrived and tried to clear the street by means of baton charges. After the fighting had died down, it was discovered that Mahomed Abdullah had been killed by a blow to his head with a blunt instrument. Four other men who had taken part in the riot also had fractured skulls. At the inquest into Abdullah's death, five white men were named as being possibly responsible for his death. However, other witnesses claimed that the death had taken place in the street, when the police were lashing out furiously with their batons. This was at least a plausible hypothesis and nobody was ever convicted of any involvement in the death.

After three days of the worst rioting ever seen in Cardiff, the police eventually succeeded in restoring order. There had been rioting in other parts of South Wales at the same time as the disturbances in Cardiff. In Barry, a man had been stabbed to death and in Newport the police had cleared the streets with baton charges. The Chief Constable of Cardiff, David Williams, was sufficiently worried that his men might lose control of the city that he had taken the precaution of asking for military assistance. A company of the Welsh Regiment had been secretly moved into the city and was ready for action. The stipendiary magistrate had been given notice that his services might be required to read the Riot Act before the soldiers went into action.

Taken together with the riot at Kinmel Camp in March, we can say with assurance that in the space of three months, there were a number of gun battles in Wales that year, generally involving colonial soldiers, either Canadians or Australians. These shooting incidents left at least half a dozen men dead from bullet wounds and many more injured. It is hardly surprising that against such a backdrop, there were plans to use the army to keep the peace.

The rioting which took place over the spring and summer of 1919 was indistinguishable from the events in other European countries at that time; with soldiers and former soldiers angry about unemployment, housing and the apparent indifference to their difficulties which was being displayed by both central and local government. There was also a good deal of animosity directed towards the police. In Britain, such actions were, by and large, ignored or dismissed as hooliganism. Let us see now what an actual abortive revolution at that time looked like and see if it differed in any material way from the kind of thing which was taking place across Britain throughout 1919.

On 21 March 1919 the Hungarian Soviet Republic was established, under the leadership of Bela Kun. From the beginning, the hope in Hungary was that Austria too would become a Soviet Republic. The two countries had, after all, been linked for many years as the Austro-Hungarian Empire. It certainly looked for a while as though Austria was about to undergo its own revolution. The Hungarian regime sent emissaries to Vienna, who worked with local Communists, hoping to unify Austria and Hungary in a single communist state. At a huge rally in Vienna of the Danube Sailors' Soviets on 17 April, there were public calls for the union of Austria and Hungary under the banner of International Communism. The following day, demonstrations and marches indicated that the revolution had begun. The Vienna correspondent of *The Times* takes up the story:

> The demonstration was begun by the unemployed, who, after holding a meeting in front of the Rathaus, sent a deputation to the Parliament House to lay their demands before the State Chancellor, Herr Renner. The demonstrators were joined by other demonstrations of repatriated prisoners and war invalids, and the mob seized a coal-cart and smashed the windows of the Parliament House with lumps of coal, firing also a number of shots against the building. Herr Renner soon afterwards arrived and told the deputation of unemployed that he could not alone accede to their demands, which were being considered by the Cabinet when he was summoned away.

So far, there is nothing here which we have not already seen taking place in an even more serious form in Britain in the same year. Remember though that this was subsequently described as an attempted revolution. The events which followed were also no worse than those seen in towns such as Luton or Cardiff: 'Subsequently a section of the mob threw matter impregnated with petrol through the broken windows of the Parliament House, and at least two rooms were completely burnt out or badly damaged. From time to time bursts of firing took place, and the total casualties are estimated at five killed and forty wounded.' It is hard to see that this abortive revolution was any worse than the rioting, arson and occasional shooting which was such a regular feature of life in Britain at that time. Indeed, since the trouble in Austria was limited to a day or two in one city, it might very well be argued that the situation in this country was a lot worse. After all, the violence in Britain, which cost more lives than the Austrian 'revolution', was spread across the whole country and lasted for months.

Things were a little fraught as the summer continued, after the gun battles in Cardiff. Whatever the mood of the army, at least the police could be relied upon to follow orders and deal with anything which they were ordered to tackle. However, into this mix of industrial action, rioting and mutiny came the worst possible news for the government, which was that in July, the police planned to go on strike. It was obvious that this could prove catastrophic. If the army could not be relied upon to obey orders and act against working men, then what on earth would happen if the police were removed from the equation? At times, such as during the disorders in Luton, the police alone had been unable to cope. Even at Epsom, they had found themselves overwhelmed, with fatal consequences. What if the police left the streets entirely now and it fell to the army, whose loyalty was open to doubt, to deal with what were seen by many in the government as incipient workers' uprisings? This is precisely what happened in Liverpool at the beginning of August 1919 and, together with the rail strike a few weeks later, it was the climax of the difficulties which Britain faced that year. Both the police strike, at which we will look in the next chapter, and that on the railways, necessitated calling upon the army for help in aiding the civil power.

Chapter 7

Purging the Police

The idea of 'purging' the police of disloyal or discontented elements sounds like something which one might expect to hear of happening in Soviet Russia under Stalin. That the British police might be purged in this way is a surprising and disconcerting idea. Nevertheless, in the summer of 1919, Sir Nevil Macready, Commissioner of Police for the Metropolis, used this very expression to describe the process which the capital's police force had undergone. Hundreds of men had been removed from the force and Sir Nevil hoped that those who remained would be loyal both to the government and their fellow officers.

In July 1919, the police in Britain were finding it just about possible to cope with the mood of rebellion which had gripped the country during the first half of the year. On two occasions, they had needed to call in the army to assist them, but generally they were able to handle things, although it was touch and go at times, as during the rioting in Cardiff in June. The reliability of the army was in doubt though, and nobody in government wished to see this put to the test by being manoeuvred into a situation where orders would be issued to troops which they might choose to disobey. This was thought to be especially likely when the orders might entail confronting strikers. If that happened, and troops refused to obey, then the consequences would be incalculable, encouraging those who wished to portray the government as weak and unable to control the streets. This was the reason that Glaswegian soldiers were not ordered onto the streets of their home city in January. Nor was it a theoretical risk; the mutinies which had been seen in Southampton, London, Folkestone and Calais showed what could happen and were thought by some senior officers to be the harbinger of worse to come. At least, in the defence of the mutineers on those occasions, it could be said that they had only refused to obey orders in peaceful situations rather than in the face of the enemy at time of war. By the summer, however, things had deteriorated and it was now impossible to say which units would or would not follow orders, even in battle.

The position in which the government found themselves, no longer able to depend upon using the army to handle either foreign wars or domestic discontent, was a direct result of the military adventure launched against Russia in 1918. One aim of the intervention had been to suppress Marxism and prevent extreme left-wing ideas being exported to Britain and causing unrest there. A very senior civil servant at the Ministry of Labour told the Cabinet in June that the real effect of British troops being sent to fight the Red Army had been the diametric opposite. Sir David Shackleton said that the industrial unrest which was sweeping Britain was in fact being exacerbated by the intervention in Russia. He told them of, 'The extent to which men of all classes were now coming round to supporting the Labour view that the Soviet government ought to be given a fair chance'. In other words, it was not only left-wingers who were now opposed to the involvement of British troops in Russia's civil war, but men and women of all political shades. There was something of David and Goliath about the new and struggling nation finding itself battling with the might of the British Empire. Combined with the indubitable fact that most people in the country were sick of war and longed for Britain to be fully at peace, all made the despatch of forces to northern Russia very unpopular.

Nowhere was opposition to the war against Russia greater than in the armed forces themselves. Very few soldiers, from commanding officers down to the humblest sailor or infantryman, really understood why Britain should be prosecuting a war against a former ally who was, as far as anybody could see, posing no threat to anybody. After surviving the hazards of the First World War, few members of the armed forces were enthusiastic about risking their lives on a mad venture of this sort, of which most of them in any case disapproved.

The lack of enthusiasm for the war in Russia was demonstrated in the most practical way imaginable by the refusal of serving soldiers and sailors to obey orders in the field. The mutinies which had taken place earlier in the year, when men who were champing at the bit to be demobilised from their units in southern Britain or France, were, by the summer, affecting the British armed forces who were fighting the Bolsheviks in Russia.

As early as February 1919, two sergeants of the Yorkshire Regiment had been court-martialled and sentenced to death for refusing to obey orders to advance on the Russian town of Seletskoe. The men had halted their unit and encouraged them to go no further, in direct defiance of orders. Neither sergeant was actually shot, their sentences being commuted to imprisonment for life. The last thing that anybody wished was to create martyrs by executing British soldiers during this most unpopular war.

In June, things became even more serious, when the Bolsheviks were on the point of being routed near the Dvina River. When the Hampshire Regiment was ordered forward to engage the Red Army; both officers and men refused to advance. Perhaps the most serious instance of mutiny to occur in the British Army on active service the twentieth century took place near Murmansk in northern Russia in early September 1919. The 6th Battalion Royal Marine Light Infantry had been shipped to the Arctic port of Murmansk for the stated purpose of aiding with the evacuation of British forces, the intervention in Russia against the Bolsheviks theoretically being wound down at this time. The marines were, however, ordered into battle against the Red Army on 28 August to seize the village of Koikori. The attack was a failure and resulted in the death, among others, of the battalion commander. A week later, there was another unsuccessful attempt to take the village, which ended in more British casualties. When they were ordered to renew the assault the next day, the entire battalion refused to fight; retreating instead to a nearby village, out of range of the guns of the Red Army The mutiny of the 6th Battalion Royal Marine Light Infantry ended with a mass court martial of ninety-three men, of whom thirteen were sentenced to be shot, although none of the sentences were carried out and all were later reduced to a year's imprisonment. It was the worst mutiny seen in the British Army for a century.

The increasing number and scale of mutinies in the army and navy were worrying for the government because they knew that a situation could very soon arise when they would be dependent upon the armed forces not only for occasional industrial disputes such as those in Glasgow and Belfast, but for the day-to-day maintenance of public order in the cities of Britain. The reason for this was simple; the loyalty of the police and their willingness to obey orders could no longer be taken for granted. In 1919, disputes between the rank and file in various forces and their senior officers was coming rapidly to a head. This clash did not appear from nowhere and had in fact been brewing for six years.

1919: BRITAIN'S YEAR OF REVOLUTION

The National Union of Police and Prison Officers (NUPPO) had been founded in 1913. For the first few years of the war, which began the following year, the union grew slowly but steadily, although they took no industrial action until 1918. Police wages had lagged badly behind the rate of inflation and there was dissatisfaction over pensions and other matters. Technically, it was a sacking offence to join the union and so it operated in some ways rather like a secret society. In August 1918, things came suddenly to a head when a police constable called Tommy Thiel was sacked for union activity. The NUPPO had never been popular with senior officers and the sacking of PC Thiel was meant to be a signal that membership of the union would no longer be tolerated. Instead, it caused the first police strike ever seen in the country. In London, 12,000 police officers walked out, leading to the use of soldiers to guard railway stations in the capital. In Whitehall, soldiers were brought in to protect government buildings from police protestors who might be minded to harm the occupants.

The demands of the strikers were comparatively modest. They required the reinstatement of PC Thiel, an increase in pay and official recognition of their union. There were those in the government who regard such an action in wartime as little short of treachery. A senior official at Scotland Yard said that the striking police officers were, 'mutinying in the face of the enemy'. Lloyd George, who was in France at the time, returned at once to Britain and acceded to every point of the programme presented to him by the leadership of the union. Every point, that is, but one: official recognition of the NUPPO. Lloyd George told the leaders of the strike that this could not be done in wartime, but that the matter would be considered once the Germans had been beaten. Many of the strikers understood this to mean that their union would be recognised when the war was over.

Given that in August 1918, nobody knew that the war had only a few months to run, one can hardly blame Lloyd George for settling the police strike as quickly as possible. Nevertheless, there were indications that there was more to the strike than met the eye. It was thought in some quarters that the police union would link up with the wider trade union movement and work in concert with other unions which were planning strikes. If so, the government might find that the police would refuse to obey instructions to tackle disorder arising from strikes such as those which had gripped Glasgow and Belfast. Lloyd George himself evidently

106

feared this to be the case, for he said after settling the police strike, 'The country was nearer to Bolshevism that day than at any time since.' Lloyd George was not alone in expressing this view. In a debate in the House of Lords in October, Lord Wittenham voiced an opinion held by many. In the process, he coined a turn of phrase which would later be used by Margaret Thatcher, when she warned of the 'enemy within' during the miners' strike. Lord Wittenham said: 'And so with the Police strike, I feel that there was something behind. I will never believe that the Police would have taken the extreme step that they took, the terrible step, unless there had been some sinister force behind that got hold of them and drove them on – the enemy in the midst and Bolshevism.'

Following the settlement of the 1918 strike, one official expressed the view that if the police union was recognised, then there would be attempts to set up similar unions in the army and navy. The leadership of the NUPPO was likened to a soviet and it was suggested that Bolshevism was at the back of their demands. One thing which was noticed by some newspaper reporters was that the police strikers in Whitehall seemed to get on very well with the soldiers sent to control them. When lorry-loads of soldiers arrived at Downing Street, the police officers held their rifles for them as the troops climbed down and everybody present appeared to be on friendly terms. Men of the Grenadier Guards, one of the regiments upon which the government would rely during the mutinies in early 1919, told observers that they would refuse to act if ordered to disperse the police officers crowded into Whitehall. Others viewed the situation quite differently.

Lord Riddell, a newspaper magnate and close friend of Lloyd George, wrote later in his War Diaries that the police strikers in Whitehall had shown a, 'very menacing attitude' and that this had made the occupants of Downing Street feel 'that they were really face to face with a revolution'. It must certainly have been disconcerting for the Prime Minister and Chancellor in Downing Street to find that these most vital public servants were now refusing to do as they were told. That troops were taking up position in and around Whitehall and Scotland Yard can only have added to the air of crisis.

It is hard, a century later, to realise what a terrible crisis the 1918 police strike represented for the government and the country. On the Western Front, Field Marshal Haig was preparing to advance on the Hindenburg Line and found, to his fury, that General Sir Henry Wilson, Chief of the

Imperial General Staff, was discouraging any major action that summer, on the grounds that troops were needed in Britain because of the police strike. Haig was not the only one to see the actions of the police union as being tantamount to treason. Just when Britain and her allies were within striking distance of winning the war, the NUPPO chose that very moment to take industrial action. It was a particularly unfortunate time for the capital to be left without anybody to maintain public order.

Wilson's claim that the need for troops on the Home Front was more urgent than any projected assault upon the Hindenburg Line was only too true. Units of the Guards set up machine guns outside the Foreign Office in Whitehall and also at Scotland Yard, whose gates were now locked. Elsewhere, public buildings had soldiers standing guard and key strategic positions in London were occupied by troops. It looked to some observers almost as though the government was preparing to defend the capital against attack by an enemy. Whether the machine guns were to be used against the police or to discourage rioters or insurgents was not clear.

It is perhaps the most basic tenet of military strategy that one does not, if it can possibly be avoided, fight on two fronts simultaneously. The priority for the Prime Minister and his Cabinet was winning the war against Germany and so it was politic, at least for the time being, to make peace with the NUPPO. At a meeting with the executive of the union, held at 10 Downing Street on 31 August 1918, Lloyd George apparently caved in at once. PC Theil was reinstated, a wage increase was agreed, pension rights were improved and a promise was made to examine the question of recognition of the NUPPO as soon as the war was over. Everybody parted amicably and it looked, at least on the surface of things, as though the police had won a famous victory over the government.

Perhaps if the members of the NUPPO executive had been a little more astute, they would have weighed the Prime Minister's words with greater care. So pleased were they at having secured their pay rise and so on, that they had perhaps forgotten what a wily old fox they were dealing with. Lloyd George had told them that, 'The government cannot recognise a union for the police in *wartime*.' The police understood this to mean, by implication, that such a step *would* be considered in *peacetime*. They had no real grounds at all for supposing this to be what was meant and it was this unthinking assumption on their part which was to lead them into disaster a year later.

PURGING THE POLICE

No government, even in the most liberal democracy, can allow police officers and soldiers to hold an allegiance greater than that which they owe the state. Such a state of affairs is a recipe for disaster, because under those circumstances there is sure to come a time when these twin loyalties will clash and a government will find that its orders are being questioned or even disregarded. Lloyd George was a shrewd man and knew this perfectly well. The time was not, in the middle of a world war, opportune to settle the question, but plans could certainly be laid in preparation for the confrontation which would surely not be too long delayed, when once military victory against Germany had been achieved.

Even as the Prime Minister was shaking hands with the representatives of the police union, he was persuading the Commissioner of Police for the Metropolis to resign. Sir Edward Henry was almost seventy and had been in the post for fifteen years. Foreseeing that a serious confrontation was inevitable in the near future, Lloyd George wanted a man in Scotland Yard who had experience of dealing with crises which might entail strong measures, up to and including the use of troops. So it was that he invited a career soldier, General Nevil Macready, to take charge of the Metropolitan Police as the new Commissioner of Police for the Metropolis. Macready, a man who detested trade unions, was, at least from Lloyd George's point of view, the ideal candidate for the post.

With the mood of unrest in Britain becoming increasingly strident, it took no great political acumen to see that as soon as the war ended, there was going to be trouble of various kinds on the domestic front. That being so, it was important to have a man in charge of the capital's police who knew how to deal with discontent. Since the army would probably be called upon to play some sort of a role in tackling any attempt at revolution, it made perfect sense to put a military man in charge; one who understood how to coordinate army and police in tandem against those who might be working to overthrow the established order. In this respect, General Macready was the ideal man for the job.

The army had been involved in tackling unrest in Britain for three years running, shortly before the outbreak of war in 1914. Macready had been at the forefront of these events and had played a key role in formulating the strategy which had prevented industrial disputes and occasional outbreaks of rioting in 1911 from escalating into a general uprising. It had been a delicate balancing act, but Macready had pulled it off by ensuring that the armed forces remained under the control of

London, rather than being prey to the whims and wishes of local magistrates.

It is sometimes forgotten that the army played an active role in British domestic affairs during the closing years of the nineteenth century, being the ultimate power upon which the state depended when things looked as though they might be getting out of hand. It was of course for this reason that there was uneasiness in 1919 about the wave of mutinies and strikes which were affecting the army, which meant that they might not be reliably ready to play their part in peacekeeping duties in their own country, should circumstances require.

In 1908, a House of Commons select committee was set up, to enquire into, 'the power possessed by Civil Authorities to obtain Military aid in the suppression of disturbance'. The committee found that the army had been called in to help the police when they were unable to cope on no fewer than twenty-four occasions between 1878 and 1908. The armed forces had helped deal with disturbances as varied as the Cornish fishing riots, the Bridgewater bricklayers' strike, miners' strikes in South Wales and disputes in Grimsby between fishermen and their employers. When the civil power called for military assistance in this way, it meant in effect that a local mayor or magistrates were able to decide what measures were needed and even when the troops could open fire.

In 1910, Major-General Macready, as he then was, was despatched to South Wales to prevent the strikes there from provoking a wave of lawlessness. Macready insisted that he and his men should not be subject to the vagaries of local magistrates, but should rather be answerable directly to the government in London. This probably helped to prevent things getting out of hand both in 1910 and also the following year, during the 'Great Unrest'. More controversially, Macready assumed authority over the local police forces as well as the army units he was commanding. He believed that only a unified approach by troops and police together could work to stifle any revolutionary activity. This then was the man personally chosen by Lloyd George to lead the Metropolitan Police in the months following the end of the war in November 1918.

The mood of increasing militancy among the trade union movement in general as 1918 turned to 1919 affected the police union. One immediate result of the apparent victory following the strike in 1918 was a huge increase in membership of the NUPPO. In August 1918, the union had had just 10,000 members. By the end of the year, this had soared to

50,000. The strike had sent a clear message to many rank and file police officers that industrial action was likely to pay dividends in the future. As 1919 drew on, even more police officers joined the union. In Sheffield, it was claimed that by the spring of 1919 346 of the 366 police officers in the city belonged to the NUPPO. Allegedly, over 90 per cent of members of the Metropolitan Police belonged to the union.

Macready believed, quite correctly, that he had been appointed by the Prime Minister to ensure that never again were the police in a position to blackmail the government by the threat of strike action. As soon as he took charge of the Metropolitan Police therefore, Macready made no efforts to compromise with the police union. Indeed, he bypassed it entirely, refusing even to recognise it, let alone to negotiate with its leadership. Instead, he set up his own representative body for the police, consisting of one delegate from each of the twenty-six London police districts. These officers were to be elected by secret ballot and were the only men with whom the Commissioner of Police for the Metropolis would deal, as far as grievances and complaints were concerned.

With the rise in industrial action which Britain saw in the first months of 1919, it seemed likely that sooner or later the police would be drawn into another strike, either for reasons relating to pay and working conditions or out of sympathy with others involved in another dispute. A general strike was a very real possibility that year and if the police union were to be called upon by the TUC to join in such a strike, there was every chance that they would oblige. It will be remembered that the NUPPO was allied to both the TUC and the Labour Party. If there was to be another confrontation between the government and the police, Lloyd George and his Cabinet wished to decide upon the timing of such an event themselves and not be taken again by surprise, as had been the case in 1918. All necessary preparations would be made beforehand. The boil of police militancy was to be lanced, but with as little disruption to the smooth running of the country as was humanly possible.

Since so many more police officers now belonged to the union than had been the case in 1918, it was felt that the first thing necessary was to make a number of concessions which would, it was hoped, have the effect of making the men less anxious to risk their jobs by striking. In March 1919, the Desborough Committee was set up to look into matters such as the pay and conditions of work of police throughout the whole country. This was in any case a much-needed step, because in some districts, the wages paid to police constables were lagging badly behind other less important occupations. The reason for the disparity of pay between one part of the country and another was that wages were set locally by the authorities in each individual county or borough. In Newcastle, for example, police officers were paid no more than street sweepers.

When Lord Desborough's committee published its report in July 1919, a number of recommendations were made. On the whole, these were welcomed by the men on the beat. The committee wanted an immediate increase of pay for all police officers, together with the provision of free housing. These new pay scales were to be implemented nationally, another recommendation being that the Home Secretary should assume responsibility for all police forces and not just the Metropolitan Police, as was then the case. All this was very welcome to the average bobby on the beat. Almost as an afterthought, the Desborough Committee suggested too the setting-up of a body which should represent the interests of police officers. This was to be instead of, not as well as, the NUPPO.

The stage was now set for dealing with the union militancy in the police force. The government announced that they intended to implement all the measures set out in the report produced by the Desborough Committee. This would be done by introducing an Act of Parliament – the Police Act. Once this was passed, membership of a trade union would be a sacking offence for police officers and it would be illegal for them to go on strike. This was the stick. The carrot was a great rise in wages and the provision of various other benefits such as free housing. Also, after twenty-five years' service, police officers would be able to retire on half pay if they wished.

Nobody had the least idea how the members of the NUPPO would take this announcement. The union had enjoyed a huge growth in numbers since the successful strike in 1918 and if these men all stood firm, then things would become very tricky. The government was banking on the likelihood that most men would be so pleased with the greatly-improved conditions of service that they would be willing to surrender their right to belong to a union in exchange for the material advantages being dangled in front of them.

For the NUPPO, there were only two choices; fight or flight. They could either call a strike and challenge the government directly or they could, on the other hand, simply surrender without a fight. So complete had been the victory when last the union called a strike, that they clearly felt that with a greatly increased membership now, they could not lose. At a meeting of NUPPO's executive committee on 31 July, a sudden and unexpected announcement was made, calling for a national police strike to begin the following day.

With the exception of one city, the national response to this, the second police strike, was wretched. In London, where the previous strike had been so dramatically successful, only 5 per cent of the men refused to parade for duty. It had already been announced that any police officer who went on strike would face instant dismissal. It was perhaps assumed that this was something of a bluff by Sir Nevil Macready in London and the various Chief Constables in other parts of the country. After all, in 1918, not only did all those taking part in the strike keep their jobs, but some sacked officers were even reinstated.

Those who believed that they could manipulate the government and persuade them to compromise had misread the situation entirely. With the army still not altogether to be relied upon, it was vital that the police would follow any orders to deal with strikes and unrest. If there were Bolsheviks in the force, they had to be rooted out. This at least was the way that people such as the Commissioner of the Metropolitan Police viewed the matter. That in hindsight those in authority were right about this and the members of the union wrong, may be seen by what happened over the August Bank Holiday in an area where the strike was fairly successful and half the police obeyed the NUPPO call for industrial action. The results of the action were little short of apocalyptic.

Before looking at the effects of the strike in the northern city of Liverpool, let us see how Macready's tough strategy worked in London and also how other parts of Britain fared. It was fairly clear that despite the claims of the NUPPO that 95 per cent of the police belonged to the union, this was a huge exaggeration. Even those police officers who were members of the NUPPO did not support the union in all its actions. The meeting of the Manchester branch of the NUPPO held on 13 June showed how many officers in England were feeling about the idea of another police strike. One speaker announced, to resounding cheers from the police officers who were present, all of whom were union members: 'There is a force somewhere in this country which is trying to lead the National Union of Police to become the thin end of the wedge for social revolution. This must not be in Manchester.' Other branches of the NUPPO reacted similarly to the idea of a national strike. They had been happy to strike for higher pay, but many members believed that they were being drawn into a political confrontation with the government, a fight in which they wished to have no part.

The strike was called on 31 July and was to start on 1 August. Once the date was announced, the government played a master-stroke. They swiftly arranged that all police officers should be given an advance on their increased pay, that very week, of £10 each. This was a considerable sum of money in 1919, equivalent to perhaps three or four weeks' wages for the average constable. For most police officers, the raise in wages was the primary consideration and this had now been achieved without any industrial action. The majority of the men were less concerned about such abstract matters as the official recognition of their union or even in establishing their theoretical right to strike, than they were in ensuring that they and their families had sufficient food on the table. There was also a keen awareness that there was no shortage of former soldiers who would cheerfully step forward to take their jobs if they should end up being sacked. It had been emphasised that all pension entitlements would also be forfeited by men who refused to report for duty on the day that strike was supposed to begin. For those who had spent ten, fifteen or even twenty years in the force, this was a chilling prospect.

When it came to the crunch on 29 July, there was very little support for the strike and what support there was, was limited to three areas: London, Birmingham and Liverpool. In London, only 1,000 or so police officers, the vast majority of them constables, went on strike. In Birmingham, 119 men out of a total force of 1 340 refused to turn up for duty; about 9 per cent. The only part of the whole country where there was any real support for the strike was in Liverpool and the neighbouring towns of Birkenhead and Bootle. In Liverpool, where there were 2,200 police officers, 907 constables and forty-eight sergeants refused to parade for duty on the day of the strike. This meant that only half the usual force was available. In the usual way of things, having only half the number of police officers on duty might not have been disastrous, but then the summer of 1919 was not at all usual. There had been chaos and disorder already across the country and a sudden and dramatic reduction in the number of police on duty was enough to trigger some of the years' most shocking scenes. We shall look at the effect of the strike in Liverpool in detail in the next chapter. Illustration 18 is of striking police officers in London in the summer of 1919.

PURGING THE POLICE

Those who withdrew their labour at the end of July had been warned bluntly what to expect. It could not really have come as a surprise to find that every single man who went on strike was immediately sacked. Not one was ever reinstated. Legally, the Chief Constables and Metropolitan Police Commissioner were perfectly within their rights to take this step. The NUPPO had played right into their hands. There had been a wish to clear out all the left-wing agitators to be found in the various forces such as London and Liverpool, but although the names of the men were known, getting rid of them wholesale would have created a lot of ill will among the rest of the men. In this way, the matter could be neatly and expeditiously dealt with: the malcontents could be deprived of their jobs on the perfectly reasonable grounds that they had flouted the oath which they had sworn on entry to the police and refused to work. There were one or two attempts at sympathetic strikes in support of the police. In London, 500 engine drivers on the London and South-Western Railway walked out and in Liverpool, there were calls for a rail strike. These efforts soon fizzled out, leaving the police strikers to stand alone.

In London, where the police strike had been something of a flop, Sir Nevil Macready issued a statement about the strike on Saturday 2 August. In it, he said:

During the last two days the force has passed through a crisis from which it has emerged with credit to itself and with an established position in the confidence of the public. That confidence was shaken by the events of August 1918, since when grievances have been rectified, and measures have been taken by the government to ensure that the conditions of pay, of pensions, of redress of grievances, and of the welfare of all ranks shall be in all ways commensurate to the importance and responsibilities of the service. That the attempt which has been made to seduce the Metropolitan Police from their duty and their allegiance to the state has failed is evident from the fact that out of a total of 19,004 all ranks only one inspector, one station sergeant, 27 sergeants, and 965 police constables have refused duty up to 6 a.m. to-day. Whatever motives may have influenced those men, the fact remains that they violated the oath they took on joining the force, and have brought disgrace upon themselves and ruin upon their dependents. The Commissioner feels sure that from this day the

Metropolitan Police, purged of these discontented elements, will not only maintain but increase the great reputation which the force has held in the eyes of the world.

After it had become obvious that the strike had failed, Home Secretary Edward Shortt addressed the House of Commons on Monday 4 August. He said: 'I can only point out that this strike is not an industrial dispute to which ordinary methods of conciliation can be applied. It is, on the contrary, a definite act of mutiny on the part of those who have broken their oaths and who are setting aside their duty to their fellow citizens and attempting to defy the authority of Parliament.' The Home Secretary also claimed that 'foreign money' was being accepted by the police union to encourage them to strike and that there was a conspiracy to 'hand over the country to the mercy of the criminal classes'. As for the proposed Police Act, whose provisions for the banning of trade unions in the police force had precipitated the strike in the first place, that was to pass through Parliament in exactly the form that had been already decided. It is to this very day illegal for the police to engage in trade union activity or to go on strike.

The national police strike had been a miserable failure, but in one place, its effects had been sensational. There had been greater support in Liverpool and the surrounding towns of Birkenhead and Bootle than in London. The sudden shortage of police officers on the streets during the strike precipitated scenes which made it seem to many that the feared Bolshevik revolution was not just round the corner, but had actually arrived.

Chapter 8

Warships in the Mersey

It was in the northern English city of Liverpool that the effects of the 1919 police strike were most keenly felt. In part, this was no doubt because a far greater proportion of officers came out in favour of the strike in that city than was the case elsewhere. It will be recalled that in 1918, the great majority of the rank and file of the Metropolitan Police walked out. This had the effect of precipitating a crisis in the middle of the war and caused the Prime Minister to capitulate almost immediately. In the summer of 1919, things played out very differently. Of the 20,000 members of the Metropolitan Police in London, fewer than a thousand took part in the strike. This was in contrast to Liverpool, where about half of the officers in the city came out on strike

There are a number of reasons for the enthusiasm of the Liverpool police for the national strike. Police constables in Liverpool at that time were earning less than general labourers and the force was famous for the strict discipline which was enforced upon junior ranks. There were formal parades, with constables being marched around like soldiers on a drill square. The problem of low pay was exacerbated by the attitude of the local Watch Committee, which insisted that police officers should live only in the 'better' parts of Liverpool. Since rents in these districts were higher than elsewhere, this tended to make officers even more short of money. They were in effect being compelled to live a middle-class lifestyle on wages which were lower than most unskilled manual workers.

That half the police force was on strike at the beginning of August does not altogether explain why Liverpool should so rapidly have descended into anarchy as soon as the strike begun. As has already been remarked, rioting and disorder often tend to occur in waves. Liverpool had already seen an outbreak of rioting a few months earlier, which had nothing at all to do with a reduction in the number of police officers on the streets. This earlier disorder might well have given some of the less advantaged citizens a taste for civil disorder and made them more ready to take to the streets when a new opportunity presented itself.

We saw in an earlier chapter that there had been a series of military riots and mutinies in Britain; some of which ended in the death of those involved in them. In 1919, public violence was never far beneath the surface and exploded for trivial reasons or none at the least excuse. This simmering discontent had manifested itself in June of that year in a series of race riots of the most savage nature. Liverpool had been in the forefront of these disturbances.

As is often the case with such apparently spontaneous outpourings of violence, there were deeper motives at work than just a trifling quarrel after leaving a public house. Something like 5,000 West Africans had come to work in the Liverpool docks during the war and a number of discharged soldiers felt that they were unable to get work because of the large number of blacks employed. It was this underlying anger which provoked the rioting, which continued on and off for the next fortnight. What were described by the newspapers as 'colour riots' were not limited to Liverpool and were, in some parts of the country, far worse. In Cardiff, for example, four men were killed when shooting broke out between blacks and whites. The *Manchester Guardian* reported that: 'Last night an altercation between blacks and whites led to the complete holding up of the docks district, revolvers being freely used and casualties caused by bullets, razors, sticks and stones.' As usual, discharged soldiers were heavily involved in the fighting. Once again, there was resentment at the large number of black men working in the docks who were supposedly taking jobs which could have been filled by demobilised soldiers.

All of which brings us back to Liverpool at the beginning of August 1919. Before the police strike even began, there was a mood of anger and defiance in the city, to say nothing of a great deal of poverty and unemployment. Even with a full complement of police on duty, rioting was apt to take place on the flimsiest pretext. It is important too to remember that trouble was still fermenting across Europe: political difficulties which were leading to street fighting and the threat of revolution. It is in this wider context that the problems in Britain must be viewed. Everywhere one looked across Europe, the threat of revolution hung in the air.

On Friday 1 August 1919, the Watch Committee in charge of the Liverpool police warned that any man who failed to parade by eight that evening would be dismissed from the force. Some members of the NUPPO were persuaded by this threat to return to work. As darkness fell, about half the police officers in Liverpool had failed to show up for duty and the mayhem began.

The rioting and looting which broke out as soon as word spread that the ranks of the police were so depleted was not in any sense politically motivated. There had already been rioting in Liverpool a few months previously and this was for many simply a chance to show the authorities what they thought of them, while acquiring free goods at the same time. It was a spontaneously outpouring of anger, with a strong business edge. The dual temptations to show contempt for the forces of law and order, while at the same time getting new shoes, bottles of whiskey or jewellery, proved irresistible.

The trouble began in Scotland Road, Byrom Street and Great Homer Street. The mob's targets were, to begin with, clothes shops, jewellers and pawnbrokers. At first, the authorities in Liverpool hoped that enrolling special constables would be enough to dampen down the disturbances. Shopkeepers and businessmen were sworn in and issued with armbands and batons, before being sent to the aid of the regular officers who were doing their best to disperse the crowds of looters. By the early hours of Saturday morning though, it was plain that more would be needed than a few hastily recruited amateurs.

At dawn, the wreckage of shop fronts along main roads showed the extent of the damage caused by the rioting. There was every prospect that with nightfall on Saturday, the looting and rioting would resume and so there was little choice but to issue an appeal for help from the armed forces. The government, fearing a complete breakdown of law and order which might prove contagious, had already ordered three warships to sail from the anchorage of the Home Fleet at Scapa Flow in the Orkney Islands. Chief of these was the mighty super-dreadnought HMS *Valiant*. With a displacement of 29,150 tons, *Valiant* was as long as London's BT Tower. The armament carried by this, one of the most fearsome warships in the Royal Navy, was formidable indeed; eight 15in guns, twelve 6in guns and four torpedo tubes. With her crew of over 900 men, she was more than a match for any other ship in the world. Now, accompanied by two destroyers, HMS *Valiant* was steaming at top speed towards Liverpool.

There were two reasons for sending a naval task force to Liverpool. One was so that sailors could be landed to secure the docks and protect them from rioters or saboteurs. This was a realistic fear, because the dock gates were actually set on fire during the second night of disturbances. This end could probably have been achieved though by using some of the thousands of soldiers who were brought onto the streets of the city over that Bank Holiday weekend. The primary purpose of mooring such an impressive ship in the Mersey, clearly visible from across Liverpool, was as a show of force. Seeing the super-dreadnought and her escort of destroyers would send a signal to both the rioters and striking police officers that the gloves were now off and the government was ready to use any means at its disposal to pacify the city.

To underline the message being delivered by the presence of warships moored near the city, thousands of troops were rushed into Liverpool on the day following the rioting. They were supported by four tanks, which were positioned on the high ground between the North-Western Hotel and St George's Hall. Troops in full battle kit, including steel helmets and with fixed bayonets patrolled the streets and stood guard at public buildings. This show of force was enough during the daytime to discourage any trouble, but when night fell, the rioting resumed. In Illustration 19 can be seen a soldier guarding a looted shop in Liverpool's Scotland Road. Tanks arriving in the city centre are shown in Illustration 20.

The first shop to have its window smashed on the Saturday night was a jewellers' near the Rotunda Theatre. Troops were rushed to the area and a magistrate read the Riot Act to the crowd. Fearing that they were about to be overwhelmed by the huge mobs, who showed no fear of them, the troops opened fire, shooting over the heads of the rioters. This quietened things down in that part of the city, but the looting simply spread elsewhere, to places where there were fewer soldiers. The troops were thinly scattered and this meant that each soldier might be outnumbered hundreds to one when a shop was being looted. One soldier stood helpless as crowds smashed their way into a clothing store and men climbed into the window and handed out fur coats to the women who were present. A little distance away, some men brought a horse and cart to a looted shop and removed the remaining stock wholesale. In Birkenhead the Riot Act was also read, by a magistrate standing in an armoured car and surrounded by soldiers.

On Sunday 3 August, General Snow of the Western Command arrived in Liverpool to take control of the troops. That morning, an appeal from the mayor was read out at every church service in Liverpool. He urged all able-bodied men to sign up as special constables for a month, in order to restore order. The situation appeared to be deteriorating and as if things weren't bad enough already, a bakers' strike had begun and the tram drivers were also threatening to stop work. Because so many working men depended upon the trams to get to their places of work, a tram strike would have caused immense problems for the entire city. There was also talk of the railwaymen coming out in sympathy for the police strike. At an open-air meeting on Sunday evening, the local branch of the Labour Party a resolution was passed, calling for a general strike to begin immediately. It read: 'That Liverpool trade unionists declare common cause with the National Association [*sic*] of Police and Prison Officers, and that in order to give immediate and necessary assistance a down tools be herewith declared. All trade unionists of this district are agreed to cease work at once on account of the attack made by the government on trade unionism.'

Having found that the soldiers were seemingly reluctant to act against them, the crowds of looters on Sunday became bolder and attacked a brewery in broad daylight. This led to the first fatality of the rioting. In Love Lane, a bottling store was broken open and men began getting drunk on the beer that was found on the premises. They were so busily engaged in this pleasant occupation that they failed to notice a lorry-load of soldiers pull up. These men had been ordered to put a stop to the looting and so arrested several men, put them in the back of the lorry and prepared to drive off. So hostile was the reaction of the crowd that shots were fired over their heads. This had no effect, because a rumour spread that only blanks were being used. A man called Thomas Howlett darted forward and grabbed a soldier's rifle. After a brief struggle for possession of the weapon, it went off, wounding Howlett in the thigh. He died in hospital the following day. An inquest later decided that the soldier holding the rifle, Lance-Corporal Seymour, was not to blame for the death. A verdict of justifiable homicide was recorded.

Elsewhere in the city on Sunday, stones were thrown at the troops, who were becoming tougher in their response to the continuing disorder. In Stanley Road, about a mile from the centre of the city, the looters began working systematically, darting forward and smashing windows and then grabbing what they could before the soldiers could get to the scene. The police also tried to intervene, but were not able to gain control of the situation. Troops fired on the crowd and one man was taken to hospital with a bullet wound to his neck. About ten at night, crowds gathered near St George's Hall, where the tanks were stationed. They began to loot shops along London Road, until a squad of soldiers first fired over the heads of the looters and then made a bayonet charge at them. Police and special constables followed, swinging their batons and managing to arrest some of the looters.

So far, much of the rioting had been opportunistic looting and stone throwing, but an hour after the bayonet charge in London Road, two soldiers standing sentry duty on the corner of Christian Street were attacked by a mob who were obviously intent upon injuring them. They responded by firing warning shots to drive away the men threatening them. A body of police officers appeared and launched a baton charge at the crowd, driving them back.

So menacing were things growing as the Sunday night drew on, that the army set up a Lewis gun in London Road. It was aimed along the length of the street, so that if need be, the area could be swept with automatic fire. In Birkenhead too, the troops were having a hard time of it and it was only with great difficulty that they managed to secure the docks. The fear was that rioters might tamper with the pump-houses or otherwise sabotage machinery. A rumour went round that the Birkenhead town hall would be treated in the same way as that of Luton, which had of course been burned to the ground during a riot a few months previously. Troops were stationed around the town hall to protect it.

On the morning of Monday 4 August, the trams in Liverpool stopped running, as a result of a strike which had nothing to do with the police strike, but was rather concerned with wages and working hours. The railway workers though were threatening industrial action in support of the police, having formed the ominous sounding Liverpool District Vigilance Committee. The *Valiant*, together with the destroyers HMS *Whitby* and HMS *Venomous* were moored off Prince's Landing Stage and sailors from all three vessels had landed and taken over the docks from the soldiers who had been guarding them. Nearly 400 people, men, women and children, appeared in court on charges relating to looting and rioting. One man asked for bail, on the grounds that he had been wounded in a bayonet charge. The magistrate was unsympathetic and told him that he would receive adequate medical treatment in the prison hospital.

To the relief of the army and police, rain began falling on the Monday evening. The old saying about rain being the policeman's best friend was neatly illustrated, because the heavy downpours discouraged people from hanging around the streets that night. The army had changed their tactics too, which also helped. Rather than being burdened with full kit, including rifles that they were reluctant to use, the soldiers had all been issued with pickaxe handles and these weapons were all that they carried on their patrols on Monday. Certain areas were declared off limits and, together with the rain, the consequence was that the centre of Liverpool remained quiet that night.

The police strike had been settled, in the most brutal and direct way imaginable; showing that Lloyd George and his government were quite prepared to take the gloves off and fight as hard as they knew how. They had also, by the deployment of huge numbers of troops and sailors, backed by warships and tanks, shown that if they were pressed, that they would use any means necessary to establish the authority of the state over anybody in the country. It was the third time that year that the military had been called out to tackle unrest on the British mainland and there could be no possible doubt in anybody's mind that the army would be brought in again, whenever necessary.

Industrial action was still bubbling away in the background though and the following month would see what was in a sense the climax of the year's unrest.

Chapter 9

The Crisis Comes to a Head

On Saturday 27 September 1919, the *Manchester Guardian* carried an exceedingly sombre editorial about an event which, it was feared, could presage a disaster comparable with the war which had ended less than a year previously: 'What will happen? Among many people there is the same sense of apprehensive bewilderment as followed the news of war in August, 1914. Is there really a comparison? Do we stand on the threshold of a civil upheaval in any way comparable with the plunge into foreign war? Or will the fundamental sanity of the nation save us from slipping into domestic chaos? No one can answer these questions.'

The previous day, large crowds had gathered in Whitehall and Downing Street, just as they had before the declaration of war in August 1914. Although they were cheering the Prime Minister and had come to support the government, so many people were crammed into Downing Street that mounted police had to be used to clear the area.

We have followed the sequence of events in Britain from the end of hostilities in 1918 to the police strike in the summer of 1919. The impression one gains is that the country was lurching from one crisis to another and each new emergency seemed to be more serious and potentially disastrous than the one before. The mutinies in the armed forces, both at home and abroad, the imposition of something approaching martial law in Glasgow, the widespread rioting which swept the country, including the death of a police officer during disturbances and gun battles on the streets of a British city, the police strike and the rioting in Liverpool; things appeared to be going steadily from bad to worse. That being so, what was it that the *Manchester Guardian*'s leader writer was concerned about in the early autumn of the year; a situation apparently thought by some to be as significant as the start of the First World War in 1914?

The railways of Britain were, as we have already observed, of far greater strategic importance to the nation than is now the case. It was for this reason that some were comparing a threat to their smooth functioning as being comparable to the threat of war in the summer of 1914. Before the outbreak of the First World War, there had been a number of separate companies operating the railways of Britain. Because of their military importance, the government nationalised the railways during the war and administered them all from London as part of the war effort. The railway unions were among the most militant, but they, like everybody else in the country, put their own personal interests to one side in the need to beat Germany. In return, the government raised their wages, although inflation ate away at the money which they received. Before the war had begun, five years earlier, railway workers had been earning roughly 18 shillings a week (90p). When the railways were nationalised, the government began paying a 'War Bonus' to those working on the railways in recognition of the hugely important role that the men were playing in the war effort. This was an additional payment of 33 shillings (£1.65) a week. This meant that in 1918, the average wage for a railway worker was about £2 11s a week, or £2.55 in modern terms. This was a decent-enough wage a century ago, but the cost of living had risen during the war by 115 per cent and so the buying power of the money had declined sharply in comparison with pre-war prices. In addition to the War Bonus, Lloyd George's government made a number of vague promises to the effect that when the war ended, they would remember the important part played by the railwaymen and this would be rewarded in some great, but unspecified, way.

However, the main object of the government which was elected at the end of 1918 when they looked at the railways was not dishing out rewards, but trying to run them more cheaply. One obvious way of achieving this end would be to see if the wage bill could be reduced. It is possible to have some sympathy for the government point of view. There was something incongruous and a little absurd about the idea of continuing to pay a 'War Bonus' a year after the war had actually ended. The railways were becoming an increasingly irksome financial burden to the government and some way of easing that burden was necessary. Obviously, with the cost of living having more than doubled, there could be no question of reducing wages to the levels which they were at in 1914: the rail unions were in a very prickly mood that year and nobody wished to provoke a strike. Lloyd George decided to ask the President of the Board of Trade to look into the question and make a recommendation on the best way forward. Sir Auckland Geddes (brother of Sir Eric Geddes) investigated and came to the conclusion that the fairest and most equitable solution was to restore the wages of men working on the railways to the level which they were at in 1914. Of course, the figures would need to be adjusted upwards to take into account the inflation since that time and Geddes came up with a weekly amount of £2. This was 11 shillings (55p) less than they were currently receiving, which mean that the 564,800 men working on the railways were, in effect, being expected to accept a 20 per cent reduction in their wages! It is perhaps hardly to be wondered at that the unions refused such a proposal point-blank.

At first, it appeared that there was some room for negotiation and during the last two weeks of September, many people were optimistic that some kind of settlement might be cobbled together. The unions themselves were not so sanguine. During the war, they had been given all sorts of assurances that the government would not forget the important work performed by the railway workers and that they would reap their reward when the fighting ended. The end of it all was that the drivers and stokers were now being told that they could expect only to return in real terms to the wages and standard of living which they had enjoyed before the war. This was hardly a reward! As J. H. Thompson, General Secretary of the NUR, put it: 'The short issue is that the long-made promise of a better world for railwaymen which was made in the time of the nation's crisis, and accepted by the railwaymen as an offer that would ultimately bear fruit has not materialised.'

The chief officers of the NUR had meetings at Downing Street on 25 September and the mood was generally optimistic. *The Times* that day appeared to be privy to information not available to anybody else connected with the confrontation, reporting that: 'In spite of some rather sensational developments of the railway dispute yesterday, including the publication of a strike ultimatum from the National Union of Railwaymen to the Government, it can be stated with some confidence that negotiations between the union and the Government will be resumed today, and that there will be no railway strike this week.'

The following day, the national railway strike began at midnight. It took no great political acumen to see that the government intended from the beginning to rely upon the armed forces in what was seen as a challenge to the state. This was not, after all, a case of a union having some grievance against a company employing its members, but of a body of over half a million men who were employed directly by the government and who proposed to disrupt the trade and industry of the whole country. At ten to three in the afternoon of 26 September, the meeting between the railwaymen and the Cabinet, held at 10 Downing Street, broke up, with an announcement immediately afterwards that the strike would begin at midnight. Two hours later, Field Marshal Haig, Commander-in-Chief of Home Forces, arrived at Downing Street, as did Major-General Feilding, Commander of the London District. The two men spent over an hour and a half attending a Cabinet meeting at which plans were drawn up for a military response to the strike.

Haig came up with an ingenious, but politically unworkable, suggestion. Many of the engine drivers and stokers were technically army reservists. Why not simply call them up and then order them, as soldiers, to drive their locomotives? The idea of undertaking what would amount to a new wave of conscription would have caused more trouble than it was worth, especially with the riots and mutinies which had already taken place that year among servicemen who were angry at being retained in the armed forces. It was already the case that all further demobilisation would have to be halted for the duration of the strike, as every soldier was liable to be needed. Announcing even a partial mobilisation at the same time would have been disastrous publicity for the government.

The great fear was that the railwaymen's strike would turn into a general strike, if the Triple Alliance became involved. Under its terms, the railwaymen could ask the miners and transport workers, including the dockers, to come out in sympathy. This would have caused the entire country to grind swiftly to a halt. As it was, even without such an appeal from the railwaymen; miners and dockers would soon be standing idle. The coal from mines was transported by rail to power stations and other places where it was needed, such as factories and steel works. It would not take long, before all industries would feel the effects of the strike. This was to say nothing of the way in which a railway strike would affect the ordinary family. We are so used to seeing huge lorries delivering food to supermarkets these days, that we sometimes tend to forget that a hundred years ago, most goods were transported not by road, but by rail. There was serious talk about the possibility of famine if the trains stopped running for long. Food rationing had partly ended, but now it was restored in full. Restrictions on the sale of petrol had been lifted at the end of the war. Now, they were brought back.

The strike which began on 26 September was the first opportunity to put into practice the ideas formulated by Sir Eric Geddes earlier that year, when he chaired the Supply and Transport Committee. The Defence of the Realm Act was invoked and the Cabinet began seriously to consider ruling the country by means of district commissioners who would be backed by the army and navy. This would be tantamount to placing Britain on a war footing and with Parliament in recess, it would give the Prime Minister practically dictatorial powers. The process was begun within hours of the railway strike beginning.

On 27 September an order was announced under the Defence of the Realm Act, which allowed the Food Controllers for a district to requisition any horse or motor vehicle which might be needed:

> The following are the provisions of the Road Transport (Requisition) Order, 1919, dated September 27th 1919, made by the Food Controller under the Defence of the Realm Regulations:
> – The Food Controller hereby orders that, except under the authority of the Food Controller, the following regulations shall be observed by all persons concerned: –

There then followed, in legal terminology, a notice to the effect that any of the twelve Food Controllers, whose names were given, had the power to declare a state of emergency and commandeer any horses, cars, lorries or vans that they might need.

Other steps were also taken by the government; preparations which they had long had in mind for just this kind of emergency. The recruitment began of 'Citizen Guards', known also as 'Civic Guards', who were to join something along the lines of the Home Guard of the Second World War. The intention was to create a paramilitary force which could aid the police and army, made up of men who were loyal to the government and opposed to Bolshevism. Over 70,000 men signed up for this organisation. The strike ended before much use could be made of these volunteers. Another Regulation was made through the Defence of the Realm Act, which rationed coal and forbade using electricity for advertising. Wasting fuel was also made an offence. The most significant preparation made for what could easily have become a general strike and organised challenge to the authority of the government was the deployment of large numbers of troops.

THE CRISIS COMES TO A HEAD

That a Field Marshal and a Major-General were summoned to the first Cabinet meeting after talks with the unions had broken down, should have been a clear indication of the direction in which Lloyd George's mind was working. As we have seen, the army were in 1919 already coming to play a major role in the affairs of the nation. From Glasgow in January, to Luton in June and then Liverpool in August, the armed forces had become the ultimate arbiters in industrial disputes, riots and attempts at insurrection. Debilitated by mutiny and discontent they might be, but the army and navy were, in the final analysis, the only power upon which the authority of the government rested. Haig had assured the Prime Minister on 26 September that there were enough loyal troops to put down any sort of uprising and frustrate any plans to institute any alternative government in Britain. This was no fantasy: there was a very real prospect that some of the militants involved in the Triple Alliance would, if they saw an opportunity, try to set up soviets which would carry out the functions more properly associated with local authorities or central government. Six months after the 1919 railway strike, the miners went on strike and a conference of ministers met to consider the danger to the state. On that occasion, Sir Laming Worthington-Evans, Minister without Portfolio, said, 'We need eighteen battalions to hold London.' The danger was thought to be that great that the capital might need to be secured by military force.

During the railway strike in September and October 1919, 23,000 soldiers were mobilised and actively engaged in supporting the government by guarding vulnerable points such as bridges, railway stations and power stations. A further eighty-six infantry battalions were on standby, ready to go into action if the situation deteriorated. Six cavalry regiments were also held in reserve. The navy was also brought in. In the Admiralty's accounts of that year of the actions in which the Royal Navy had been involved, there were the expected theatres of war such as the Baltic and North Russia, but there was also a heading for 'Assistance to the Civil Power'. This revealed that ten destroyers, twenty minesweepers and six sloops had been in action in September and October in British waters. Parties of sailors had been landed to secure docks and power stations and protect them from saboteurs. On 29 September, five torpedo boats arrived at Greenwich. Three were from Chatham and two from Portsmouth. More than 500 sailors were landed, including stokers, who were then taken by lorries to an unknown destination. At the northern fishing port of Grimsby on the same day, sailors were put ashore from a destroyer, so that they could operate the dock gates.

The military actions were being guided and coordinated by the Strike Committee chaired by Minister of Transport Sir Eric Geddes. It was this committee which examined the various ideas being put forward by senior officers for ending the strike swiftly. Sir Eric did not think much of Haig's scheme for recalling to the colours railwaymen who happened to be reservists. Nor was he at all keen on a suggestion from an admiral, to the effect that the Royal Navy had many ratings who were stokers and could be used to drive trains during the strike. Replying to this proposal, Sir Eric said, 'Some naval ratings could operate a locomotive, but none are likely to possess experience enough to drive a train.'

Every branch of the armed forces was keen to show that they alone could help the government in tackling the crisis. Even the Royal Air Force tried to get in on the act, by claiming that their airship *R-33* could carry 10 tons of coal from Bedford to East Fortune near Edinburgh. This was yet another scheme which the Strike Committee did not think worth implementing. The city of Liverpool was a worry to Sir Eric, in view of the serious disturbances there in August, which had only been put down by troops, backed by tanks, opening fire on the crowds and by the arrival of a naval task force. The army assured Sir Eric that there were three battalions within eight miles of Liverpool ready to go into action.

Quite apart from the more fanciful and far-fetched schemes for carrying coals to Newcastle, or Edinburgh, by airship, the military had a serious and important part to play in handling the strike. Some trains were still able to run, by using men who did not belong to either the NUR or the other railwaymen's union, the Associated Society of Locomotive Engineers and Firemen (ASLEF). The sight of any train running or signal box operating infuriated the strikers and they expressed their displeasure vigorously. On Sunday 28 September, a train left Waverly in Scotland, heading for Aberdeen. Between Kirkaldy and Thornton, it was pelted with rocks and stones. One of these struck the fireman, who was gravely injured. There were between 300 and 400 passengers on the train at the time. If the driver had been put out of action by being hit by a rock, the potential death toll would have been enormous. Another train travelling from Anstruther to Edinburgh was also attacked and many of its windows smashed. Signal boxes were also stoned in the West of Scotland

In England, things were growing even more dangerous. On the same day that the trains were stoned in Scotland, attempts were made to derail two trains in the south of England. At Pulborough in Sussex, flat stones were placed on the tracks and at Warnham, also in Sussex, boulders were rolled onto the line. After these two acts of sabotage, the army were called in to patrol the line. Nor were these the only incidents of violence. Soldiers were sent to Yeovil in Somerset, where disturbances were reported. Meanwhile, in Surrey, a company of soldiers in full battle gear were guarding the railway junction at Woking. Troops wearing steel helmets and carrying rifles took up positions by bridges and signal boxes. Wolverhampton also saw a nearby railway junction being occupied by the military.

Some newspaper correspondents remarked that driving through Britain at this time put them in mind of France during the First World War, there were so many lorries on the roads carrying troops. Heavily-armed soldiers left their base at Aldershot and began guarding Aldershot and Farnham railway stations. In London, an army camp was established in Hyde Park and troops took up positions at Waterloo Station and other termini. One installation which was heavily guarded by the military was the Lots Road power station in Chelsea. This was the biggest power station ever built, with a generating capacity of 50,000 kW. It consumed over 700 tons of coal every day and provided the electricity for the whole of the London Underground, as well as much of the tram network. Anybody managing to stop operations at Lots Road would have closed down the a large part of London's transport system. With the railways on strike, protecting the Lots Road power station from harm was vital if those living in and around the capital were to be able to get to work. A company of soldiers secured the perimeter and stood guard day and night, ensuring that nothing was allowed to interrupt the smooth running of the place.

There was anxiety in some quarters about the possibility of soldiers fraternising with the pickets of strikers who were standing outside stations. Certainly, there seemed to be no animosity between the strikers and the troops and there was friendly conversation between the two groups at times. It was noticed that at Waterloo Station, the striking railwaymen seemed to be on very amicable terms with the soldiers on duty. In Glasgow, where there had been a well-founded fear in January 1919 that local soldiers might have gone over to the side of the strikers, the same expedient was adopted during the railway strike as had been during the industrial action by engineers nine months earlier. Instead of

131

calling upon soldiers from the Glasgow barracks at Maryhill, units of the Argyle and Sutherland Highlanders were brought to the city to guard the railway lines and stations.

Little wonder that the Commander-in-Chief of Home Forces, Field Marshal Haig, was too busy at this time for any ceremonial or social duties. On Thursday 2 October, Haig was due to visit Wolverhampton, where he was to receive the honorary Freedom of the Borough but the engagement was cancelled. The day before he was expected to visit Wolverhampton, the news came that trains running in Scotland were to start carrying armed guards, with instructions to take 'effective measures' if anybody tried to interfere with the running of the railways. This followed more instances of stone-throwing at trains in Scotland.

So far, the army had only been involved in the strike in a passive way. They had marched into position, were standing guard at railway stations, patrolling lines and being deployed at strategic junctions. It had not been found necessary actually to order any soldiers to do more than this. It was their very presence which was intended to deliver a message to anybody minded to create mischief. Although the government was quite prepared, if it came to it, to use military forces in a more active way; they hoped to avoid this if possible. It was nevertheless the case that there was a need for men who would help out against the strikers by driving vehicles, aiding in the supply of food, patrolling sites where strikers might cause damage and in many other ways as well. Despite the 'purging' of the police which had been undertaken a couple of months earlier, there was still the suspicion that the rank and file of the various police forces, being almost wholly composed of working-class men, might feel some sympathy for the striking railwaymen and lack enthusiasm for breaking their strike. There were also still thought to be many militant trade union men in the police and it was not known how they might react to any orders regarding strike-breaking. What were needed were reliable, middle-class men who were angry at the inconvenience of the railway strike and eager to put a stop to it.

One of the recommendations made by the Supply and Transport Committee when it had been established earlier that year under the chairmanship of Sir Eric Geddes, was to set up an organisation which would allow right-thinking men to come to the aid of the government against Bolshevism and the threat of sedition and unrest. These had been provisionally called 'Citizen Guards'. Nothing much had been done about the idea, but now seemed the perfect time to set in motion the creation of such a body. The whole scheme was fraught with difficulties and had the potential for precipitating a class war, but just before midnight on 3 October 1919, the government issued the following proclamation, which was published in national newspapers.

> In the opinion of his Majesty's Government the circumstances of the present crisis are such that special measures should be taken to secure the liberty of all peaceable citizens and to protect them in the pursuit of their ordinary work and of the special work undertaken to maintain the supply of food and other necessaries to the community.
>
> The numbers of the regular police forces and of the existing small forces of special constabulary are insufficient for this purpose. The government, therefore, invite all lords lieutenant, lord mayors, mayors, chairmen of country councils, chairmen of standing joint committees and watch committees, and chief constables, town clerks, and other local officers to take steps for the formation in all counties, cities, and boroughs of citizen guards to undertake to act in co-operation with the police in the duty of protection and maintenance of order. They request that in each county, city, and borough the officers above named should form forthwith a committee for the organisation and recruitment of such a citizen guard.
>
> If the food and the existence of the nation are to be safeguarded in face of the menace by which they are confronted today, it is essential that all citizens who are willing to contribute labour should be allowed to do so without interference or apprehension. The government therefore appeals to all well-affected men to come forward in order that they may assist to preserve and guarantee the security of those without whose continued and unmolested exertions the life of the nation cannot be maintained.

The tone of this statement was enough to raise eyebrows and set alarm-bells ringing in some quarters. It could be interpreted as a call to arms, an appeal for men loyal to the established system, as represented by Lloyd George's government, to sign up and be prepared to do battle. This is certainly how the *Manchester Guardian*, a famously liberal and

133

progressive newspaper, chose to take the call for 'Citizen Guards'. It was remarked in an editorial that this sort of thing could easily be seen as the beginning of a class war. The strikers were working class and volunteers for the citizen guards overwhelmingly likely to belong to the middle class. The *Manchester Guardian* expressed the fear that expressions 'Citizen Guards or 'Civil Guards', might evoke the image of the White Guards, the armed militias who were fighting the Bolsheviks in the Russian Civil War. Their existence might motivate left wing workers to organise themselves as 'Red Guards'. Others, thought this fanciful. After all, the government had only asked for men to come forward to 'contribute labour' and ensure that supplies of food were maintained.

As a matter of fact, the Citizen Guards, known also as the Civil Guards, were a good deal more sinister than just being a kind of special constable of the sort that proved so useful during the war. The government were not being altogether open and honest about their intentions, although there were hints. The Prime Minister received many telegrams on the day after issuing the appeal for volunteers and over 70,000 men signed up to the scheme. From 10 Downing Street came the information that the primary purpose of the new force would be to relieve the army from the guard duties which they were currently undertaking at strategic and vulnerable positions. The armed forces should ideally, thought the government, be held in reserve.

No secret then, was made of the aim of having the new volunteers take over some of the duties which soldiers were engaged in during the railway strike. There was far more to it than that though. Four months after the call for volunteers, as a new wave of industrial and social unrest threatened the stability of the United Kingdom, a special conference of ministers met to discuss both the planned industrial action and the possibility of a revolution taking place in Britain. The meeting on 2 February 1920 was attended by, among others, the Prime Minister, Winston Churchill, the Chief of the General Staff, the Home Secretary Edward Shortt, the Lord Privy Seal Andrew Bonar Law, the Minister for Munitions Lord Iverforth, the First Lord of the Admiralty W. H. Long and the Minister for Labour Sir Robert Horne. These were the men who ran the country and that day they were engaged in discussions about how best to put down any unrest by force of arms. The discussions at this meeting almost defy belief and give a stark insight into the true nature of Lloyd George's government at that time.

Winston Churchill and the Chief of the General Staff thought that the country was almost defenceless. The RAF was, for example, able only to keep 100 aeroplanes in the air at once. Lloyd George ventured to suggest that these 100 planes were still able to fire machine guns and drop bombs. That the threat being debated was internal and did not relate to attack by a foreign power was made clear in the conversations which followed. The First Lord of the Admiralty said that, 'The peaceable manpower of the country is without arms . . . a Bill is needed for licensing persons to bear arms.' Home Secretary Edward Shortt replied rather testily that, 'The Home Office had a Bill ready but in the past there have always been objections.' At this point Bonar Law, Lord Privy Seal and soon to be Prime Minister, expressed his opinion on the best way of tackling strikers and the menace of internal dissent. He said, 'All weapons ought to be available for distribution to friends of the government'. The Minister for Munitions explained helpfully, 'We have a surplus of all kinds of munitions. We have been selling them to the Baltic states.' Sir Robert Horne, Minister for Labour, wanted to get Chief Constables to prepare secret lists of reliable men who would aid the government in a confrontation.

We must be very clear about what was happening here. The coalition government of Lloyd George was talking of arming one section of the population to fight against another; in short, preparing for civil war. It is in this context that the recruitment of the so-called 'Citizen Guards' in October 1919 must be seen. They would not merely be standing guard on bridges to replace the army sentries: there was a definite desire on the part of senior members of the government that they should also be given weapons to use against the enemies of the government.

The question to which nobody knew the answer during the early days of the railway strike was whether or not the NUR and ASLEF would appeal to the miners and transport workers to come out in sympathy. Had they done so, thus activating for the first time the dreaded Triple Alliance, then there is no saying what might have happened in 1919. Certainly, instead of remembering as we do today, the General Strike of 1926, we would talk of the 1919 General Strike. The consequences of such a strike in that year would have been incalculably worse than was the case in 1926. The army were still unreliable and so too were the police. It is no wonder that the government wished to form a militia of reliable men who would be prepared to bear arms against any attempt at revolution.

1919: BRITAIN'S YEAR OF REVOLUTION

The Citizen Guards, which were to be raised in October 1919 were the direct descendants of the Yeomanry, who proved so useful in suppressing disorder in the years following the Napoleonic Wars. It was the Yeomanry cavalry who inflicted such terrible casualties at St Peter's Fields in 1819. The Yeomanry were really a bit like the modern Territorial Army: volunteer, part-time soldiers who could be called up in an emergency. Since the Yeomanry were all expected to provide their own horses, they belonged almost exclusively to the middle classes; there were no working men among the Yeomanry. They were a body of middle class men dedicated to maintaining the status quo. This is roughly what the Citizen Guards would have been, had the crisis in the autumn of 1919 deepened and turned into a general strike.

Fortunately, eight days into the railway strike of 1919, the government blinked. Had they not done so, it is impossible to say what might have happened. As it was, a compromise measure was put forward, whereby payment of the War Bonus was to continue for the next twelve months pending a full review of the situation. By agreeing to allow the existing pay arrangements to continue for another year, both sides were able to claim victory and neither the unions nor the government were humiliated. This was of the utmost importance. The General Secretary of the NUR, J. H. Thomas, put the matter in a nutshell, echoing what Lloyd George had told the miners' leaders earlier that year. The railway strike, like that which the miners had planned, would be in effect an attack on the state. This was because both industries had been nationalised during the war and remained under control of the government. Thomas expressed the opinion that any strike against the state must be a disaster, whatever the outcome. If the strike was successful, then the state would be defeated, with dangerous implications for the unity of the nation. If, on the other hand, the strike failed, then industrial democracy would be the loser. It was for this reason that it was in everybody's best interests to present the outcome as not being a victory for either side in the dispute.

It will be recalled that Field Marshal Haig had cancelled his visit to Wolverhampton, where he was due to be given the freedom of the borough, due to the railway strike. Once it was over, his visit was rescheduled and he arrived in the city on Thursday 16 October 1919. There had been a lot of speculation that year about the possible future role of the British Army in the affairs of the nation, with particular reference to their use for strike-breaking and peacekeeping. Haig took the opportunity to make his own views on the subject perfectly plain. To place this speech in context, we must remember that across Europe various former military heroes, generals among them, were putting themselves forward as potential saviours of their nations in peacetime. In Poland, Marshal Pilsudski, the Commander of the Polish Legion, was being hailed as the natural leader of the nation and in Germany, both Hindenburg and Ludendorff were jockeying to become the most important political figures in their country. There were those in Britain who believed that a man like Haig was of the same mould. The Field Marshal used his speech at Wolverhampton to discourage any such thoughts and remind people that the army was not and should never be, a political force. Talking of the railway strike and the fact that he had been compelled to postpone his visit to Wolverhampton, Haig said: 'We were busy owing to the strike, but I am proud to think that the soldiers had not to be called upon at all. It is not our job. We exist to fight an external and not an internal foe. That reminds me to say that I hope you are getting on with the Civic Guards; they are the fellows who ought to turn out when they are wanted on such occasions.'

The mockery to which Haig has been subjected since the 1960s tends to blind us to the role he played in stabilising the country in the years following the end of the First World War. In 1965, almost fifty years after the Great War was over, Charles Carrington reflected on his own memories of those times in his book *Soldier from the Wars Returning*. Recalling the regimes which sprung up following civil conflicts in other European countries in the 1920s and 1930s, he mused upon why nothing of the kind had happened in Britain, writing of 1919 that 'Throughout the spring and summer while the Peace Conference was sitting at Versailles, criticism of the government by liberals and socialists, labour troubles, and continued unrest in the base camps, produced just the situation which a Popular Front might have promoted an agitation to sweep away the government.'

When a man who had recently retired as Professor of Commonwealth Relations at the Royal Institute for International Affairs makes such a claim, we should take it seriously. One only has to look at what was happening in Germany at this time to see what kind of danger Britain might have faced. There, demobilised soldiers sometimes drifted into associations and clubs of ex-servicemen which were fronts for paramilitary groups. These units, the *Freikorps*, were key players in the fighting which put an end to any hopes of a Soviet republic in Germany. Communists and right-wing militias battled it out on the streets. There was nothing to stop the same thing happening in Glasgow and London after the war; after all, there were many organisations for former soldiers, most with a particular political slant. This is where Haig's influence was so beneficial.

The two chief associations to which ex-soldiers belonged in 1919 were opposites in every way from a political point of view. On the one hand, there was the National Federation of Discharged Soldiers and Sailors (NFDSS). This was a left-wing group which was only open to rank-and-file soldiers. Officers were explicitly forbidden from becoming members. The other main association of former soldiers was the Comrades of the Great War. This was much more to the right and was the group to which officers belonged. The Comrades of the Great War were an extremely patriotic and loyalist organisation, with some links to the Conservative Party. There were other groups, such as the National Union of Ex-Servicemen, but these were on the whole very left-wing, leaning towards communism.

Just as with the German Spartacists and the *Freikorps*, there was the possibility of these associations of ex-servicemen turning into armed groups, struggling to impose either communist or far-right ideologies during the upheavals seen in Britain from 1919 onwards. That they did not do so is attributable in large measure to the efforts of Haig. Both the NFDSS and the Comrades of the Great War invited Lord Haig to be president of their groups. He declined, politely but firmly, telling both that he would only agree to become president if the two organisations merged into one body open to all. In June 1919, the NFDSS agreed to admit officers and the Comrades of the Great War agreed in principle to the two groups, polar opposites politically, joining together. It took another eighteen months, but eventually the Comrades and the NFDSS became what we know now as the British Legion, an apolitical, non-partisan group for promoting the welfare of former servicemen and women. Without Haig's patient diplomacy, it is by no means certain that this would have been achieved.

Keen though Haig was upon the idea of the 'Citizen Guards', others saw them as a potential menace which could exacerbate the divisions which were at that time threatening to tear society apart. On 10 October, Commander Joseph Kenworthy, the Liberal Member of Parliament for Hull, gave a speech at Walthamstow in East London. He warned that the

Citizen Guards might bring about the very thing which they were intended to prevent: the outbreak of a class war. He said: 'The proper people to keep order and protect life and property are the trained police, assisted, if necessary, by the army. An undisciplined body of amateur guards might do more than anything else to influence class hatred and cause the people to forget that, after all, we are all Englishmen who love our country.'

The fears expressed by Commander Kenworthy were much the same as those which the *Manchester Guardian* had mentioned in a leader which indicated reservations about the whole scheme. At a time when working-class men and women were in regular conflict with the government, employers, the police and even, from time to time, the army, it was hard to see how a militia made up of thousands of middle-class men could do anything other than aggravate the existing tensions.

Lloyd George and many of his Cabinet, including the Home Secretary, were of course Liberals. They could not afford to ignore criticism from their backbenchers like Joseph Kenworthy. The *Manchester Guardian* was at that time practically the voice of Liberal England and their opinion too counted for a great deal. In any case, by the end of 1919, the immediate crisis appeared to be over and the Citizen Guards had become an irrelevance. On 23 December, Home Secretary Edward Shortt announced in the Commons that the scheme for the formation of the Citizen Guards had now been abandoned. This was not quite the end of the Guards, but for the time being, it was felt to be politically expedient to drop them, at least publicly.

Disbanding the Citizen Guards before they had even been properly formed was a very neat piece of back-pedalling by Lloyd George and his Cabinet. In the early days of the railway strike, *The Times* carried a piece which began 'The formation of a Citizen Guard, we are requested to state, is not purely a strike measure, but is to have some degree of permanence.' The piece went on to give the name of the man who would be heading the organisation in the Metropolitan area, General Woodward, and various other details of how many men would be enrolled and the way in which they would be classified. It was also mentioned that the overwhelming majority of those signing up were former soldiers.

The disbanding of the Citizen Guards, before they had even had a chance to parade or show what they were capable of, is just one more example of the way in which all sides to the various disputes and confrontations during 1919 drew back at the last moment from the edge of the abyss. We saw that when the miners and railwaymen were toying earlier that year with the idea of a general strike, the leaders of the Triple Alliance were told bluntly that they were in a position to take over the state. At this point, they backed down. Similarly, during the railway strike in October, it was open to the government to force an even more serious industrial confrontation, one which would have entailed the use of the army and navy to break the strike. At the last moment, they veered away from this action. So it was with the Citizen Guards. One possibility would have been to forge ahead with the formation of what amounted to a paramilitary force of men determined to uphold the existing social order. This would, as the *Manchester Guardian* had observed, have been an invitation for left-wing elements to recruit their own 'Guards' and for the two opposing forces to square up to each other on the streets of Britain's cities. This, after all, was precisely what was happening in other European countries at that time. As it was, the government simply dropped the whole scheme in order to lower the temperature.

Another scheme which was being dropped at roughly the same time was the attempt to destroy the Bolshevik regime in Russia by military force. Despite the intervention of the Allies in the civil war which followed the Bolshevik seizure of power, there was no sign of Lenin and his followers being defeated by the so-called 'Whites'. Quite the opposite in fact. As the years passed after 1917, the Bolsheviks consolidated their grip upon the country until it was clear that they were there to stay. For men like Winston Churchill and Sir Henry Wilson, this was quite irrelevant. The struggle should continue. Their objections to communism were ideological and therefore impervious to circumstances. For Prime Minister Lloyd George, however, pragmatism was all. If the Soviet Republic in Russia was here to stay, then obvious an accommodation would have to be reached, an arrangement which was as advantageous to Britain as possible.

British naval action was still being taken against Russia in the Baltic throughout the summer of 1919. On 17 August, for instance, an attack by Coastal Motor Boats was launched against the naval base of Kronstadt; in the Gulf of Finland, less than 20 miles from Petrograd. The assault was supported by simultaneous bombing raids carried out by the RAF. Of the eight boats which took part in the action, three were lost, but the cruiser *Pamiat Azova* was sunk and two battleships seriously damaged. Any possible uncertainty about the question of whether Britain was or was not at war with Russia was ended when Commander Claude Dobson and Lieutenant Gordon Steele were both awarded the Victoria Cross for their bravery. The VC can of course only be awarded for actions, 'in the face of the enemy'.

Without consulting his Secretary of State for War, however, Lloyd George had come to a decision about the fighting in the Baltic and Arctic Oceans. While Winston Churchill was still thundering on in Parliament about the prospect of the final defeat of Bolshevism, Lloyd George delivered a speech at London's Guildhall which cut the ground away from under Churchill's feet. Churchill, who was present, was visibly shocked when the Prime Minister stood up on 8 November and calmly announced that 'We cannot of course, afford to continue so costly an intervention in an interminable civil war. Our troops are out of Russia. Frankly, I am glad. Russia is a quicksand.' Lloyd George also mentioned the huge sums of money which had been spent in prosecuting the campaign against Russia, giving a figure of £100 million. All this was a clear public statement of the British government's intentions, as well as a stinging and public rebuke to his Secretary of State for War, who was sitting a few feet away.

This speech, which clearly signalled the Prime Minister's views on future relations with Russia, was to act as a catalyst for perhaps the most serious threat to Britain's stability for centuries. For all the talk of revolution which made the government and the middle classes so uneasy that year, there was no credible and organised revolutionary movement in the country. True, there were many dissatisfied men who relished any opportunity to demonstrate their feelings about the established political system; by means of strikes, riots and mutinies. Each of these events, though, was disconnected from the others. Whatever people like Basil Thomson, Director of the New Home Intelligence Department, might claim to the Cabinet, there was no overall master-plan for sedition and revolution. The real threat to the internal security of the country was to come from an altogether different direction. As a direct consequence of the speech that Lloyd George made in November 1919, a number of high-ranking army officers and politicians, together with a very senior police officer, were to engage in a conspiracy which could have brought down the Prime Minister and even ended in a military coup. This plot, like most of the political troubles which had cropped up in the first two years following the end of the war, was inextricably bound up with Britain's dealings with the fledgling Soviet republic in Russia.

Chapter 10

The Plot to Bring Down the
Prime Minister

We have followed some of the most tumultuous and alarming events in twentieth-century British history throughout the course of the first complete year after the end of the First Word War. While the rest of Europe was racked with revolutions and civil wars, Britain managed to keep its society on an even keel, just. The death toll from the riots and mutinies which took place in this country that year probably did not exceed twenty or thirty men. This was trivial compared with the bloodshed in certain other countries, for example Germany. We should not deceive ourselves that it was the wisdom and good sense of Britain's leaders which saved us from the unthinkable consequences of the overthrow of the established order. Left to their own devices, there were those in the army and even the government who would have taken the most injudicious and provocative steps to deal with the industrial confrontations that year. Winston Churchill, who had been newly appointed Secretary of State for War, had a particularly robust view of the best way to tackle strikers.

Churchill's natural inclinations when it came to dealing with what he saw as subversion and incipient rebellion by the workers could easily have precipitated a disaster. As Home Secretary in 1910 and 1911, he had been called upon to deal with disturbances in the mining districts of South Wales which resulted from strikes there. In 1914, Lloyd George reminisced about Winston Churchill's plans during that time for tackling the strikes and disorder. He said: 'Winston then had a plan to shut the Welsh miners into their valleys by a military cordon and to starve them out. A mad plan. He had all the country planned out for a military campaign. I shall never forget the remarkable scene which I witnessed at the Home Office. Winston with his generals, and his plan of campaign.'

This intemperate man was in the Cabinet throughout 1919, plotting military adventures against the wishes of the Prime Minister. The following year, he and Sir Henry Wilson, overall commander of the British Army, went even further and engaged in a conspiracy to replace Lloyd George, on the grounds that he was too sympathetic to the Bolsheviks in Russia, perhaps even secretly a Bolshevik himself! Churchill thought that the time might have come when he could supplant Lloyd George and claim the Premiership.

By the spring of 1920, it was plain to everybody that Lenin and the Bolsheviks were going to be ruling Russia for the foreseeable future. However little personal affection he might have had for the creed of Marxism, Lloyd George knew that one way and another, Britain would have to rub along in the new world order which had emerged following the end of the First World War. The Soviet Republic of Russia was no more to his liking than an independent Ireland, but both were likely to be facts of life and so it was a matter of making the best of things. Which was presumably why, just two months after giving the speech at the Guildhall indicating that Britain's support for the enemies of the Bolshevik regime was at an end, Lloyd George went to a meeting of the Allied Supreme Council and suggested that they end the blockade of Russia which had been instituted after the Bolsheviks seized power. The Supreme Council had been founded to coordinate the Allied war effort. Between 14 and 16 January 1920, the Council, based at Versailles, agreed with the British proposal and issued a statement announcing that negotiations with the Russians would begin, with a view to normalising relations, restoring trade links and lifting the blockade.

It is by no means impossible that these moves helped to bring about the collapse of the anti-Bolshevik forces. At the very least, the possible recognition of their regime by the Western Powers must have given the Bolsheviks much-needed encouragement. Certainly, by May, the Red Army was struggling less and had begun an offensive which led to their advancing on Warsaw. That month, Lenin's government sent a delegation to London which, it was hoped, could hammer out a trade deal with the British. The negotiations were originally to have included other members of the Allied governments, but nobody other than Britain appeared to see any advantage in forming ties with the new Soviet Union. The French, still annoyed about the Russian repudiation of debts, refused even to send a representative.

Since Russia was more or less bankrupt and had few goods that Britain might want, we must ask ourselves what the real purpose of this hoped-for 'trade agreement' might really have been. The answer was simple and had nothing at all to do with trade. Lloyd George wanted the Russians not to engage in subversion and hostile propaganda against British interests, either in this country or elsewhere. In return, the Russian regime would be accorded a degree of respectability by being recognised by Britain. In other words, this was purely a matter of *realpolitik*. Lenin did not trust Lloyd George any more than the British Prime Minister trusted him. But both men could see the chance of getting something he wanted from the other.

Before the first talks were held with the Russians on 31 May 1920, the Foreign Secretary Lord Curzon briefed the Cabinet about what the real situation was, stripped of polite verbiage. He said that it was known 'that the Russian government is threatened with complete economic disaster, and that it is ready to pay almost any price for the assistance which we – more than anyone else – are in a position to give. We can hardly contemplate coming to its rescue without exacting our price for it, and it seems to me that price can far better be paid in a cessation of Bolshevik hostility in parts of the world important to us, than the ostensible exchange of commodities.' In short, trade would be quite irrelevant to any trade agreement which might be signed!

The main threat which the communist government in Russia had always posed to Britain lay in the ideas which they were promoting and, in effect, exporting. Just as in Regency England it was believed that Revolutionary France was setting a bad example to working people in Britain and furnishing them with dangerous ideas, so too with Soviet Russia in the years following the First World War. There was no doubt that having the example of the Russian soviets had helped stir up revolution in other European countries and also given a worrying pattern for strikers and discontented workers in Britain to emulate. Lloyd George's idea was that if the Russians simply tended to their own affairs and stopped encouraging revolution elsewhere in the world, particularly in those places where Britain had an interest, then Britain might in turn recognise the Bolsheviks and maintain normal diplomatic relations with them. This was a tempting prize for the Russians; that the mighty British Empire might acknowledge the legitimacy of Lenin's rule over the country. All that they would need to do in return would be to steer clear of Britain and her overseas possessions.

THE PLOT TO BRING DOWN THE PRIME MINISTER

Lloyd George's probable motives have been examined in this way, so as to make sense of the extraordinary moves a made less than three months later by the Chief of the Imperial General Staff, Sir Henry Wilson, promoted to Field Marshal in July 1919. To summarise: Lloyd George was no more enamoured of the Bolsheviks than Churchill, but saw an opportunity to curb some of their more troublesome activities at little cost to Britain. It need hardly be remarked that this new line drove Winston Churchill absolutely mad. Earl Beatty, the First Sea Lord, observed succinctly at the time, 'Winston is in despair and nearly off his head.'

The negotiations which finally resulted in the signing of the Anglo-Soviet Trade Agreement lasted for the better part of a year and it was to be 16 March 1921 before both sides were completely satisfied with the terms. For the British, the key paragraph read as follows:

(a) That each party refrains from hostile action or undertakings against the other and from conducting outside of its own borders any official propaganda direct or indirect against the institutions of the British Empire or the Russian Soviet Republic respectively, and more particularly that the Russian Soviet Government refrains from any attempt by military or diplomatic or any other form of action or propaganda to encourage any of the peoples of Asia in any form of hostile action against British interests or the British Empire, especially in India and in the Independent State of Afghanistan. The British Government gives a similar particular undertaking to the Russian Soviet Government in respect of the countries which formed part of the former Russian Empire and which have now become independent.

There were a number of bumps along the road to the signing of the treaty and it was one of these which caused three or four of the most influential and powerful men in the kingdom to toy with the notion of overthrowing the government and seizing power, perhaps at the point of a gun.

As Secretary of State for War, Winston Churchill's most important subordinate was Sir Henry Wilson, the man in overall charge of the entire British Army, both in this country and throughout the world. Wilson shared Churchill's loathing for Bolshevism and was as enthusiastic as his political master for any scheme which would help overthrow the government of Russia. By the early summer of 1920 though, Britain had withdrawn support for the White armies and they were being so comprehensively routed that the Red Army was now poised to take the newly-independent Poland, something which even Lloyd George would have been unable to tolerate. Like Churchill, Wilson watched in horror as the Prime Minister, as he saw it, set out to woo the Soviet Republic and accord it official recognition. After the Russian delegation arrived in London it looked all but inevitable that Britain and the Soviet Republic should become trading partners and, if not friends, then at the very least, no longer exist in enmity. The Chief of the Imperial General Staff began to entertain a terrible suspicion. Could it be that Lloyd George was really a Bolshevik who was intent on betraying his own country?

Two things happened in August 1920 which brought Sir Henry Wilson to the point of forgetting his proper allegiance to the democratically elected government and trying to replace the Prime Minister with a man more after his own heart. Before looking at what happened to bring about what could have been a coup by the armed forces, it is important to bear in mind that no Prime Minister of the twentieth century enjoyed anything like the democratic legitimacy that Lloyd George had had since the general election of 1918. The coalition of which he was the leader had won no fewer than 478 seats, giving them an unassailable majority in the Commons of 229. By way of comparison, Tony Blair's landslide victory in 1997 gave him a majority of just 179.

In the opening weeks of August, it looked as though the Red Army was sweeping inexorably onwards towards Warsaw, and that Poland must soon fall. This would have meant that the Bolsheviks would hold power right up to the German border. With the politically unstable state that Germany was in at that time, this would have posed a serious threat to European interests. Thinking back to the idea of the Domino Theory at which we looked in Chapter 1, it would mean that Germany and then France might fall to Marxism. Only the Channel, according to this reading of the situation, would then separate Britain from the Bolsheviks. Such a state of affairs would have been unthinkable, even to Lloyd George, who was still trying to finalise the trade agreement with Russia. Reluctantly, he hinted that if it looked as though Poland's independence was in jeopardy, then he might have no choice but to despatch the British fleet to the Baltic.

As soon as the possibility was mooted publicly that some sort of action might be taken in defence of Poland, the TUC and the Labour Party organised a 'Council of Action'. A statement was issued, saying that, 'the whole industrial power of the organised workers' would be brought to bear if Britain tried to mount any action against the Russians. It was clear that any attempt on the government's part to intervene in the war between Russia and Poland would lead to a crisis; with strike action a likely outcome. There had already been one incident in May, when a ship was being loaded with arms for Poland. The SS *Jolly George* was unable to sail due to the actions of the London dockers and eventually, the weapons on board had to be unloaded. The last thing that Lloyd George wanted just at that time was another clash with the unions. He therefore backtracked with great dexterity and on 10 August, announced in the House of Commons that there would definitely be no armed intervention in defence of Poland.

With the Polish army fleeing in a rout and the Red Army pushing on and seemingly certain to take Warsaw, Lloyd George was really just making the best of things. It was hardly worth exacerbating the terrible industrial scene in Britain for the sake of a foreign country and it was also important to British interests to secure a cessation of subversive activity on the part of the Soviet Republic. The news that no action would be taken to prevent Russia from occupying Poland and the Ukraine shocked Churchill deeply. Then something happened which made everything ten times worse. The British intelligence services had been secretly intercepting telegrams being sent to Russia and also listening to and decoding radio messages being sent between Moscow and various countries in Europe. These revealed that in the first place, Russia had been subsidising Labour's official newspaper, the *Daily Herald*, to the tune of tens of thousands of pounds. Secondly, and extremely embarrassingly for the Prime Minister, a member of the delegation discussing the Anglo-Soviet Trade Agreement had been heavily involved in the setting-up of the Council of Action which was threatening a general strike if Britain interfered in the war against Poland. All this information was leaked to the British press by both the Admiralty, who had been listening to the radio messages in Europe, and also those decoding the telegrams in Britain.

Lev Kamenev, head of the Moscow Communist Party and Commissar for Foreign Trade, had arrived in the summer to join the delegation in London which was thrashing out the Anglo-Soviet Trade Agreement. He kept in touch with Moscow via coded telegrams. Unfortunately for him, the intelligence services were intercepting and decoding these communications and they revealed that Kamenev was playing a very devious game. On the one hand, he and the other members of the Russian team were agreeing to call a halt to subversion against British interests, while on the other, Kamenev was helping to set up the same kind of councils of action in Britain as those which had been seen in Russia before the revolution. Lenin himself was complicit in these actions, urging Kamenev to 'inform the workers' in Britain about various matters. One fairly typical telegram which was sent to Kamenev in August 1920, came from G. V. Chicherin in Moscow and contained direct instructions from Lenin that the Soviet representatives in Britain should use all their powers to explain to the British workers the true situation regarding the Russian invasion of Poland.

Churchill was not the only one who was astonished and angry when it came to light that even while they were talking to the British government, the Bolsheviks were stirring up trouble by encouraging strikes in this country. Henry Wilson was of course furious with the Russians, but it also appeared to him that the Bolsheviks must have friends in high places in Britain to be able to get away with this flagrant interference in the country's affairs. Obviously, thought Wilson, the answer, horrifying as it was, was that Lloyd George himself must secretly be a Bolshevik. The Chief of Staff had, after all, sent very blunt messages to Lloyd George, which the Prime Minister had chosen to ignore. In one of these, Wilson had warned that the trade delegation 'while enjoying the hospitality of England, are engaged, with the Soviet Government, in a plot to create red revolution and ruin this country'.

On 18 August, Wilson, who, we must never forget, was the overall head of the whole British Army. confided his suspicions to the Secretary of State for War. He wrote in his diary that day, 'Winston was much excited. He said it was quite true that LG was dragging the Cabinet step by step towards Bolshevism.' The fact that the Chief of the Imperial General Staff was on such intimate terms with the Secretary of State that he referred to him by his first name is significant. The two men were more like friends than anything else. Indeed, in other references to Churchill in Wilson's diary, there is a slightly patronising air, as though he feels that it is the Secretary of State for War who is under his authority, rather than the other way round.

It is apparent that Wilson was now talking behind the Prime Minister's back to a number of other influential men, both in the army and elsewhere. Among these were Basil Thomson, Director of the New Home Intelligence Department and in charge of the Special Branch, and also Hugh Trenchard, the officer who dealt so decisively with the Southampton mutiny. Trenchard was of course something of a protégé of Winston Churchill's. In 1919, shortly after he had suppressed the mutiny in Southampton, Winston Churchill sent for Major-General Trenchard, as he then was, and after congratulating him on the way that he tackled the trouble in Southampton, offered him the post of Chief of the Air Staff. This placed Trenchard in overall control of the RAF. He was promoted later to Air Marshal, the first person ever to hold the rank and then given a baronetcy. Over the next ten years, Trenchard forged the Royal Air Force into the fighting force which did so much to win the Second World War against Germany. Not for nothing is he known today as the 'Father of the RAF'.

On 24 August, the Chief of the Imperial General Staff made an entry in his diary which is so shocking that later biographers omitted it when writing about that period in Sir Henry Wilson's life. He wrote:

> I told Winston that it was the chance of his life to come out as an Englishman and that in one bound he would recover his lost position and be hailed as saviour by all that is best in England. I think I have got him pretty well fixed. I warned him that we soldiers might have to take action if he did not and in that case his position would be impossible. He agreed. He said he was 'much worried' about LG's attitude and so am I, and it will take some explaining to ease my mind of the suspicion that LG is a traitor. Trenchard with whom I discussed this matter later, thinks, like Basil Thomson, that LG is a traitor.

This passage must rank as one of the most extraordinary documents ever to come to light from that period. We must be very clear about what is going on here. The head of the British Army is talking to the head of the RAF, the Director of Intelligence and the Secretary of State for War and canvassing their views on the loyalty to his country of a Prime Minister with a greater majority in Parliament than had been seen in living memory. He is also threatening that the army, of which he is in overall command, might take action against the Prime Minister. It is also interesting to note the patronising, almost contemptuous, way in which the Chief of the Imperial General Staff refers to his superior, the Secretary of State for War. The casual statement that, 'I think I have got him pretty well fixed', combined with the use of Churchill's first name, suggests that Wilson had little respect for Churchill and hoped to see him as Prime Minister only because he would be an easy man to manipulate.

As far as Churchill is concerned, there is not the least doubt that he viewed himself as the Prime Minister in Waiting, and was looking for a chance to take over from Lloyd George. Although he was unsuccessful on this occasion, Churchill was mixed up in another round of plotting the following year, which came closer to achieving this goal. There is something eerily prescient about Sir Henry Wilson's idea of Churchill being, 'hailed as the saviour' of the country. This is, after all, pretty much what happened twenty years later, during the Second World War.

We cannot, at this late stage, ever hope to know what was really going on in the mind of Sir Henry Wilson when he made such an entry in his private diary. Menacing as the statement 'I warned him that we soldiers might have to take action' is, there is an outside chance that it referred not to direct action by the armed forces under Wilson's control, but to something considerably milder. Some months later, Wilson was again angry about the direction in which government policy appeared to him to be heading. This time, it was the granting of independence to Ireland, of which he disapproved. He tried to persuade a large number of senior officers to offer their resignations simultaneously, in order to force Lloyd George to change tack. Even the First Sea Lord, Admiral Beatty, was approached. There was no great enthusiasm on anybody's part for a mass resignation and so Wilson dropped the scheme.

After speaking to Sir Henry on 24 August, Churchill sent a memorandum to the Prime Minister and several other members of the Cabinet the next day. He said:

> I feel bound to bring to the notice of my colleagues the perturbation which is caused to the British officers who are concerned with this intelligence work when they see what they cannot but regard as a deliberate and dangerous conspiracy aimed at the main security of the state unfolding before their eyes and before the eyes of the executive Government without any steps being taken to interfere with it. In these circumstances the

Government might at any time find itself confronted with disclosures and resignations which would be deeply injurious.

Since details of the intercepted messages between Moscow and various representatives of the Soviet government abroad had already been leaked to the newspapers, this memo looked rather like a threat to some of those who read it.

The course of events now depended to a large extent on what happened in Poland. If, as Churchill and others feared, Warsaw was to fall to the Red Army, then there would be a clear and grave threat to Germany, which had already suppressed more than one attempt to set up Soviet republics. What was to stop the Russians, once they had taken Poland, from pressing on West? In this case, the British would almost certainly be obliged to go to war again and this would inevitably have the effect of fatally weakening Lloyd George's position as Prime Minister. In early August, 1920, it looked as though that was precisely what was about to happen.

Throughout the summer of 1920, the Polish army retreated in disorder from the advancing Russians. By 12 August, the Red Army was at the gates of Warsaw and under the command of Mikhail Tukhachevsky, began to surround the city. However, in a brilliant counter-attack the Polish leader Marshal Pilsudski drove back the Red Army from the banks of the River Vistula and inflicted terrible casualties. The Russians were routed, with 10,000 soldiers killed. By 25 August, it was apparent to the rest of the world that the Red Army would not be operating in Europe for the foreseeable future and Lloyd George's policies were thoroughly vindicated. This wholly unexpected defeat for the Bolshevik army strengthened Lloyd George's position and showed that he had been justified in his handling of the situation. It was also a blow to Churchill's hopes of being seen as the man of the moment; the far-sighted statesman, whose hour had come. The Prime Minister had a quiet word with the leader of the Russian delegation, as a result of which Kamenev returned to Moscow. The Anglo-Soviet Trade Agreement was signed a few months later.

Lloyd George's pursuit of a policy of détente with the Bolshevik regime in Russia caused great strains in the relationship between him and his Secretary of State for War. Churchill had been convinced that the time was approaching which would justify his aggressive policy towards the

151

new Soviet Republic and provide him with the necessary excuse to deploy the armed forces in Europe. After the Battle of Warsaw, Churchill retreated in something of a sulk and his letters to the Prime Minister became increasingly distant and formal. At one time, the two men had been fairly close and Churchill would address his letters to, 'My dear David'. As the months passed those, he restricted his salutations to, 'Dear Prime Minister'.

It seemed that although his discussions with Sir Henry Wilson, when he had been encouraged to 'come out as an Englishman' and be hailed as 'saviour of all that is best in England', had come to nothing, Churchill still nursed the idea that he could replace Lloyd George as Prime Minister. In February 1921, he was moved from the War Office and given the relatively minor post of Secretary of State for the Colonies. This demotion, as Churchill saw it, rankled and that summer, having been passed over for the post of Chancellor of the Exchequer, he was at the centre of a new conspiracy to unseat Lloyd George and replace him as Prime Minister. On 23 June, the *Manchester Guardian* reported that Lord Birkenhead, formerly F. E. Smith, and Winston Churchill had been engaged in a plan to force Lloyd George into retirement. Lord Riddell wrote in his diary that he had been told that the *Manchester Guardian*'s story was perfectly accurate. His informant was none other than the Prime Minister's mistress, Frances Stevenson. He wrote: 'The plot was to prevail upon LG to resign on the grounds of his health and to appoint Winston PM. This however resolved itself into a scheme to appoint Birkenhead. This change led to the defection of Winston and the break-up of the cabal.' Shortly after this episode, Churchill entered what some called his 'Wilderness Years'. It was to be twenty years before he was once again to be in the running for the Premiership.

Chapter 11

The Aftermath

If a revolution, in the sense of a popular uprising, were to have been on the cards in Britain in the years following the end of the First World War, then 1919 was the year in which it would have taken place. It is a matter of historical record that it did not, either because the social and political conditions in this country were unfavourable to such a project or, more probably, for the simple reason that ultimately neither the government nor the various factions ranged against it wished to see the country precipitated into what must inevitably have been a period of chaos and bloodshed. Things were still uncertain and hazardous in the years which followed, but fortunately for the unity of the nation, a series of external threats emerged during that time, which tended to distract a little from the idea of an internal war between the classes. There was also a sharp rise in unemployment, which, surprisingly, acted to discourage industrial militancy.

In many ways, the early 1920s saw the emergence of the society which we know today, in which wars abroad and the threat of terrorism occupy our minds far more than the idea of overthrowing the government in a bloody revolt. A look at one or two of the notable events between 1920 and 1922 will give some idea of the mood in Britain at that time and explain why thoughts of revolution were receding.

Britain had been fighting a war in Afghanistan and was now militarily involved in Iraq. The Third Anglo-Afghan War of 1919 had ended in what was ostensibly a victory, but there was still the fear that Russian influence in the area was growing. The war in Iraq was driven by a simple matter of geo-political importance; the oilfields of Mosul, which Britain was determined to control at all costs. Winston Churchill, as Secretary of State for War, prosecuted the campaign enthusiastically, authorising the use of the RAF to bomb the insurgents into submission. The wars in Afghanistan and Iraq had demonstrated clearly that Churchill had been right in his claims that Britain would require a large post-war army to police her overseas possessions.

If the idea of Britain fighting, in quick succession, wars in Afghanistan and then Iraq seems familiar to us today, then the menace of terrorism will strike an even greater chord. The sight of the barrier blocking off Downing Street from the rest of the world and the armed police officers guarding it is still a strange and unsettling one for many people. They remember with fond nostalgia the time when anybody could wander along Downing Street and be photographed standing outside Number 10. The threat of terrorism has put an end to those innocent days. It has been quite forgotten though that the barrier across Downing Street and the armed police on guard duty were around long before Margaret Thatcher and the fear of IRA attacks in the 1980s.

For the victory celebrations in 1919, the architect Sir Edwin Lutyens designed a plaster and wood 'cenotaph', which was erected in Whitehall. A cenotaph is simply an empty tomb, which is meant both to symbolise those dead who have no known resting place, while at the same time referencing the empty tomb from which the risen Christ left behind. So popular was Lutyens' cenotaph, that he was commissioned to recreate the structure permanently in stone: this became the Cenotaph with which we are all familiar. It was unveiled on Remembrance Day, 11 November 1920.

Because enormous crowds were expected to attend the celebration of Remembrance Day in 1920, the war having only been over for two years, certain precautions were taken to control the tens of thousands of people who would be lining Whitehall. The fact that the newly-built Cenotaph was to be unveiled that day also caused the authorities to plan for very large crowds. Some side streets were blocked off, to enable the police to restrict the numbers who had come to pay their respects to fallen comrades and relatives to manageable levels in Whitehall. As part of these crowd control precautions, a wooden barrier was placed at the St James's Park end of Downing Street.

The situation in Ireland, which was still at that time a part of Britain, was deteriorating and the threat of terrorism increasing. Terence MacSwiney, a member of Sinn Fein and also the Lord Mayor of Cork, had earlier that year been convicted by a court martial of possessing seditious articles and documents. He had been sent to London's Brixton Prison to serve his sentence of two years imprisonment. After going on hunger strike, he had died at the end of October 1920. MacSwiney's death was the trigger for a wave of terrorist attacks in England and Scotland. This activity caused the police, both in London and the provinces, to begin arming themselves. Many of the IRA sympathisers on the British mainland were carrying guns and showed that they would not hesitate to use them. It was also suggested that the IRA might be about to embark upon a campaign of assassinations, aimed at prominent members of the government and senior army officers.

On 26 November 1920, an eight-foot high wooden barrier was built, which blocked the entrance to Downing Street from the Whitehall end. Proper foundations were dug for this defensive structure, which included gates for vehicular access. It stood in precisely the same place in which the modern gates to Downing Street are now to be found. Uniformed Metropolitan Police officers stood guard at the barrier. These men had army webbing belts around their waists, to which were attached holsters containing revolvers. This was a shocking sight to the people of London, who were used to the idea that their police force was historically unarmed. It was the beginning of what became known as the 'IRA Scare'.

This external threat to the safety and security of not only the Cabinet, but also ordinary men and women going about their business, came at an extraordinarily opportune time for Lloyd George. Only a year earlier, troops had been on guard in London against subversive elements among English strikers. Now, the menace was from an outside agency and the efforts of his government could be directed against terrorists from the other side of the Irish Sea, rather than strikers in London and Glasgow. The IRA activity which began that year was a gift from the Gods.

The campaign of shootings and arson which began in 1920 and lasted until the establishment of the Irish Free State two years later is another of those parts of British history which have been all but forgotten. At its height, many police forces in Britain were arming themselves and factories, shops, woodyards, farms and private homes were being regularly destroyed in England and Scotland. One or two examples of the sort of actions being taken might illustrate how the situation became seen as a serious emergency which distracted attention from things such as industrial action by miners and so on.

The arson attacks began in Liverpool docks on the night of 27 November 1920, when at least eighteen separate fires were started simultaneously in warehouses and wood yards. Five men were arrested and the other suspects escaped after shooting at the police. On the same night, a group of Irishmen were arrested near a timber-yard in London. They were carrying cans of petrol and revolvers. On 2 January, 1921, Police Constable Henry Bowden was shot as he attempted to question a group of men loitering near a grain store in Manchester. On 15 January, a group of IRA sympathisers tried to burn down the Vacuum Oil Works in York Road, Wandsworth and the following night a railway signal box in Barnes was attacked. The terrorist campaign gathered pace during the spring of 1921, causing the Metropolitan Police to establish the first 'Armed Response Vehicles'. These patrolled London, in an attempt to catch the IRA in the act. Meanwhile, armed officers visited potential targets in the suburbs. Major fires were started in Manchester and in Liverpool; armed police officers stood guard at power stations and bridges. On 9 March, thirteen fires were started in Liverpool and two weeks later a police officer checking the Manchester United football ground was shot at by men who had evidently been planning to set fire to the buildings there. Four days later, a total of thirty-eight fires were started at farms in Yorkshire, Durham and Northumberland. In early April, there were more arson attacks in central Manchester and another police officer was shot. Also in April came a police raid during the course of which there was a gun battle between armed officers and the IRA suspects they were trying to arrest. Sean Morgan, who was firing at the police with a pistol in each hand, was killed, the first person to be shot dead by the police in England in the twentieth century. The terrorism, which escalated until it entailed the use of high explosives as well as arson and shooting, carried on throughout 1921. In May, a police inspector was shot dead in Glasgow. The following month there was a gun battle in Bromley, South London, between the police and Irish militants. In April 1921, in the midst of this terrorist campaign, came the threat that the Triple Alliance would call a General Strike.

In 1919, the *Manchester Guardian* had compared the threat of a railway strike with the outbreak of war in 1914. Two years later, the prospect was regarded more phlegmatically. Newspapers no longer treated the possibility of widespread strike action as being the prelude to the Apocalypse. There were a number of reasons for this, not least of which was that there was so much else going on, both on the domestic front and internationally, that a series of strikes simply didn't appear to be as menacing as it had been in 1919. As the years passed after the

THE AFTERMATH

Bolshevik seizure of power in Russia and there was no sign of any other communist-backed revolutions being successful, so the idea of anything of that sort happening in this country appeared increasingly fanciful.

The other key factor at work in suppressing disorder was the recession which had begun in 1920. Unemployment was rising and jobs were becoming exceedingly scarce. We are most of us familiar with the Great Depression of the 1930s, but already in 1921, ordinary people were beginning to fret about the possibility of being thrown out of work and being dependent upon the dole. The Insurance Act of 1921 introduced the payment of so-called 'Uncovenanted Benefits', to which a strict means test was applied. In May 1921 the rate of unemployment in Britain reached the highest rate it has ever been: an astounding 23.4 per cent of the working population were out of work. This was about four times the level of unemployment at the end of 1919.

One might on the face of it suppose that such a catastrophic rise in the number of men out of work would cause a corresponding increase in revolutionary sentiments among the British working class, but in fact, the opposite happened. As more and more men were losing their jobs, those who were still in work became desperate to hang onto their jobs. When one's wife and children are at risk of going hungry, there is often less time available for toying around with radical politics. Still less do men wish to hazard their jobs by going on strike.

The next few years saw changes in government, including the first-ever Labour government and various political and industrial upheavals, culminating in the 1926 General Strike. That the strike lasted only nine days was a consequence of the government having learned well the lessons of 1919. The armed forces had proved very useful that year in showing that the government meant business and in discouraging lawlessness and disorder. In 1926, both the army and navy were used to full advantage in breaking the strike of the miners, railwaymen, dockers, transport workers, printers and steelworkers. No fewer than 80,000 troops were deployed across Britain and this was in addition to fourteen battleships and fifty-five other Royal Navy vessels. This overwhelming force meant that the strike had little chance of success and was one of the reasons why it was called off after little more than a week. The mood of the country had in any case changed since 1919 and the General Strike of 1926 was a peaceful and largely easy-going affair, quite unlike the fierce confrontations which had been seen seven years earlier. One observer at the time remarked that the strike was conducted like a Victorian Sunday morning, although without the church. Relations between the police and the strikers were often affable, as in the cases where special constables engaged in football matches with teams of strikers.

The world had also changed somewhat in the years between 1919 and the General Strike. In 1919, the most reliable way of transporting food and other goods around the country was the railway system. The idea of inexperienced people being able to operate steam engines was fairly absurd. It will be recalled that when it was suggested that naval stokers might, at a pinch, be able to get a steam train moving, there was no enthusiasm for the such a scheme, even amongst those anxious to find ways of breaking the railwaymen's strike. By 1926 though, there were many motor lorries, as well as private vehicles. These could be driven by anybody and made the stoppage on the railways, at least to some extent, irrelevant.

It is interesting to look at the subsequent lives and careers of some of the people whose activities have been chronicled in this book. Who better to begin with than the man who was Prime Minister for the whole of 1919, David Lloyd George? After being turned out of office in 1922, Lloyd George never regained power, although he did lead the Liberal Party for a while. There were those who thought that his behaviour as Prime Minister veered towards the dictatorial. When he visited Germany in 1936 and endorsed Hitler's leadership, it was seen by some as an indication of his essential character and political beliefs. Even a visit to Dachau Concentration Camp did not damage his admiration for Hitler; whom he described as 'Germany's George Washington'.

What of the other main players on the British political scene at that time? Whether by coincidence or design, the three main conspirators who were trying to remove Lloyd George as Prime Minister in 1920, were none of them in positions of authority eighteen months later. Churchill was the first to go, being moved from the War Office to the office of Secretary of State for the Colonies. At about the same time, six months after the talk of Lloyd George being a Bolshevik traitor, Director of Intelligence Basil Thomson was sacked by the Prime Minister in person for a supposed breach of security. Finally, Sir Henry Wilson himself resigned at the end of 1921, in order to enter Parliament.

Winston Churchill's later life and achievements are so well known that we need not go into them in detail. He became Prime Minister at a crucial period in Britain's history and guided the country to victory over Germany. Likely to be less familiar to the general reader is the fate of the man with whom Churchill had so much in common and with whom he intrigued against Lloyd George during 1919. Field Marshal Sir Henry Wilson, who worked with Churchill to try and maintain a large standing army in the post-war years, retired from the army in February 1922. That same year, he was elected as Member of Parliament for North Down. On 22 June, that year, Sir Henry Wilson unveiled a war memorial at London's Liverpool Street Station. He was followed home by two Irishmen, Reginald Dunne and Joseph O'Sullivan. Outside his house in Eaton Place, the two men shot the retired soldier dead. Two police officers and his chauffeur were wounded by gunfire during the assassination. Wilson's killers were later hanged.

Lord Haig's death was more peaceful than that of the man who had once been his colleague. After retiring from the army in 1920, Lord Haig spent the next eight years in working for the welfare of ex-servicemen, becoming the president of the newly-formed British Legion, among other things. He died of a heart attack in 1928 and his funeral attracted hundreds of thousands of mourners.

We saw that General Hugh Trenchard was given the task of dealing with the mutiny at Southampton in January 1919 and that he was ready and willing to shoot down the mutineers in the process, although matters did not actually reach such a pass. His later career was a glittering one and he is known today as, 'The Father of the RAF'. Churchill appointed him Chief of the Air Staff in 1919 and for the next ten years or so Trenchard built up the Royal Air Force. In 1927, he was appointed Marshal of the Royal Air Force; the first person ever to hold the rank. In 1931, Prime Minister Ramsay MacDonald asked Trenchard to become Commissioner of Police for the Metropolis; a post which he held for four years. Trenchard died in 1956, at the age of eighty-three.

Perhaps the saddest story of the later years of those who held important posts in the service of Lloyd George's post-war government is that of Basil Thomson. After having been peremptorily dismissed by Lloyd George, perhaps partly as a result of his becoming involved in plots to remove the Prime Minister from office, the one-time Director of Intelligence was at something of a loose end. In 1925, at the age of sixty-four, Basil Thomson was arrested in Hyde Park after dark and charged with 'outraging public decency' with a young girl called Thelma de Lava. Foolishly, when approached by a police constable, Sir Basil gave a false name. It was unlikely that even the greenest of police recruits would have failed to recognise the former Assistant Commissioner and Director of Intelligence. At this point, a clumsy attempt at bribery was attempted.

When the case came to court, Sir Basil Thomson claimed to be writing a book about vice in the West End of London The fact that Thelma de Lava was actually a prostitute lent some support to this defence; except that, as the police testified, 'He was violating public decency . . . sitting on a park bench with his arms around the woman's neck . . . and all that . . .' The magistrate felt that such behaviour was perhaps not altogether in keeping with the notion of a respectable man collecting information for a book and he fined Sir Basil Thomson £5. It was a tawdry end to a glittering career.

The lives of some of those who were seemingly so bitterly opposed to the existing system in 1919 make for interesting and occasionally surprising reading. David Kirkwood was prominent in the 'Battle of George Square' in Glasgow, on which occasion he was badly beaten by the police and then arrested for inciting a riot. At this time, Kirkwood was renowned as one of the fieriest militants to be found on the Clydeside. Who would have thought that such a man would go on to become first a Member of Parliament, then a Privy Councillor and finally end his days as Baron Kirkwood of Bearsden? His comrade, Willie Gallacher, also later became an MP.

Perhaps the most intriguing changes in fortune were those which befell Emmanuel Shinwell. Shinwell was of course sent to prison in Glasgow in 1919, for inciting a riot. Elected to Parliament in 1922, Shinwell went on to serve as Minister of Fuel and Power in Clement Atlee's administration after the Second World War, in which capacity he oversaw the nationalisation of the coal industry. He was then appointed Secretary of State for War and then Minister of Defence. In 1965 he became a Companion of Honour and was then created Baron Shinwell, dying in 1986 at the age of 101. It was an amazing progression, from feared communist rabble-rouser to national treasure.

Epilogue

Why have the startling and unprecedented events of 1919 been almost wholly forgotten today? Mention industrial unrest during the years between the end of the First World War and the start of the Second in 1939 and all that most people will recollect is that there was a General Strike in 1926. The Great Depression might also rate a mention. It would be rare to find anybody who knew about the violence on the streets in 1919 and the mobilisation of thousands of troops that year for peacekeeping duties in Britain. This is strange, because never in Britain's history has there been a year quite like 1919. It was without doubt a far more perilous and eventful year than any other between 1918 and 1939. Yet how is this momentous year generally recalled today, even by historians themselves?

In *The Oxford History of Britain*, described by *The Sunday Times* as, 'without doubt, the standard one-volume history of Britain', there is a single sentence about the extraordinary series of events which took place in this country in 1919. We read of Lloyd George that: 'His government used tough methods, including emergency powers and the use of troops as strike-breakers, in dealing with national strikes by miners, railwaymen, and many other workers (including even the police) in 1919-1921.' And that, as far as the most violent and eventful peacetime year in twentieth-century British history, is that.

The explanation is probably quite simple. The First World War and the Second World War were such significant periods in this country's history that they tend overwhelmingly to dominate our view of the century in which they occurred. It has been observed that whereas most centuries in British history are identified and classified by monarchs and the dynasties to which they belonged, the twentieth century is chiefly defined not by the names of kings and queens but by the two great wars which took place. We think of the sixteenth century as the Tudor period and the nineteenth century as the Victorian Age, but the twentieth is the time of the First and Second World Wars. Most people in that century framed important events in terms of, 'before the war', 'after the war' or 'between the wars', as the case might be.

Following the greatest slaughter that the world had ever seen, it is the signing of the Armistice in 1918 and the peace treaty in 1919 which tend to be remembered. The upheavals a few months later which resulted in only a few dozen deaths fade into insignificance when compared to the wholesale massacre of millions of young men at the Somme and other dreadful battles. The First World War came to such a satisfying conclusion too, with the signing of an Armistice taking place on the eleventh hour, of the eleventh day, of the eleventh month, which makes it sound as though it was just in the nick of time! It rather takes the edge of this neat and tidy ending of a major war if we then discover that within forty-eight hours of the signing of that famous Armistice, elements of the British Army were in open rebellion and that before the peace treaty had even been drawn up, tanks were being deployed in the second-largest city in Britain. We expect to find the strange-looking and cumbersome tanks of that time to have been engaged in the Battle of Cambrai, not rumbling through the streets of Liverpool and Glasgow, menacing British workers!

There is a natural human tendency to seek patterns and to prefer simple, linear narratives to complicated and messy stories which are difficult to untangle. Relating historical events in twentieth-century Britain to the two world wars makes the century more coherent and gives us a readily comprehensible framework to make sense of what was happening. A simple instance of this process, whereby we try to connect everything to the great wars which took place in the first half of the twentieth century will make this clearer.

Ask anybody in Britain about a Prime Minister between the two world wars who used the expression, 'Peace in our time' and you are sure to be told that it was Neville Chamberlain on his return from Munich in 1938. So powerful is the grip of the narrative which has been constructed that this seems indisputable. Of course it was Neville Chamberlain! Who else could it have been? The advantage of associating this phrase with the Munich Conference is that we know then that this was something to do with appeasement and, by extension, the Second World War. Of course 1938 was the year before that war actually began, which makes it is easy to remember.

It was of course not Neville Chamberlain in 1938 at all, but rather Stanley Baldwin, speaking in the House of Commons on 6 March 1925, who used the phrase 'Peace in our time' during the course of one of the most famous speeches he ever gave in Parliament. Chamberlain actually used the phrase 'Peace *for* our time' thirteen years later, but he was really only echoing Baldwin's prayer for 'Peace *in* our time'. This trivial misunderstanding sheds light upon our distorted view of British history, especially in the twentieth century. Prime Minister Stanley Baldwin was talking about *internal* peace, peace on the industrial front in Britain. Since this has no reference at all to either world war, it tends not to stick so readily in our collective memory as Chamberlain's speech on his return from Munich.

What were the chances really of a revolution breaking out in Britain in 1919 and overthrowing the Monarchy and the rest of the established order? That such a thing *could* have happened is indisputably true. That it did not is also a fact. The truth is, all parties in the various confrontations which took place that year backed down in the end, rather than force any issues to their ultimate and perhaps bloody conclusion. This was the case with both the government and the unions with whom they were in conflict. When Lloyd George admitted frankly to the leaders of the miners' union in the early part of that year that they were stronger than his government and in a position to defeat the state; they backed fearfully away from taking such a step. Similarly, when the government had the power to crush the railway strike in September 1919, they too preferred a fudged compromise. At every crisis, common sense prevailed, albeit sometimes at the very last moment. It was as though all those involved in the troubles that year, came to their senses and when once they realised where their actions might be leading, chose to halt and seek instead for some deal which would avoid catastrophe. The historian A. J. P. Taylor summed the matter up neatly with regard to the unions and their militancy, when he said of that period: 'Most socialists talked of class war, though without any serious intention of using more violent weapons than the strike and the ballot box.'

It is curious and more than a little disconcerting to note that the most deadly threat to the stability of the British state in those first few years following the end of the war came not from firebrand union leaders, but rather from pillars of the establishment such as the Chief of the Imperial General Staff and the Secretary of State for War! While the unions were arguing openly and publicly with Lloyd George's government, Winston Churchill and Sir Henry Wilson were, behind the scenes, engaged in a conspiracy which looked very much like the preliminary plans for a military takeover. In fairness though, they too stepped back from the brink and chose to let the old system muddle on as it had done in the past. In the final analysis, nobody wished to see the o_d order overthrown and a new and untested system, whether run by socialists or soldiers, take its place.

This then was the last time in its history that Britain flirted with the idea of a violent overthrow of the state, either by Bolshevik revolutionaries or a cabal of senior army officers. It is unlikely in the extreme that the curious set of circumstances which gave rise to such a situation will ever be repeated, which allows us the luxury of viewing Britain's year of revolution as being, in the final analysis, no more than an historical aberration.

Bibliography

Allen, Hubert Raymond, *The Legacy of Lord Trenchard*, Littlehampton Book Services, 1972.

Aughton, Peter, *Liverpool: A People's History*, Carnegie Publishing, 2008.

Boyle, Andrew, *Trenchard; Man of Vision*, Collins, 1962.

Brewer, Paul, *The Chronicle of War*, Carlton Books, 2007.

Brogden, Michael, *On the Mersey Beat; Policing Liverpool Between the Wars*, Oxford University Press, 1991.

Bunyan, Tony, *The History and Practice of the Political Police in Britain*, Julian Friedmann Publishers, 1976.

Calwell, Charles E., *Field Marshal Sir Henry Wilson Bart – His Life and Diaries*, Cassell, 1927.

Carlton, David, *Churchill and the Soviet Union*, Manchester University Press, 2000.

Collier, Martin, and Pedley, Philip, *Germany 1919-1945*, Heinemann Educational, 2000.

Geary, Roger, *Policing Industrial Disputes; 1893-1985*, Cambridge University Press, 1985.

Gilbert, Martin, *A History of the Twentieth Century*, HarperCollins, 1997.

Hattersley, Roy, *Borrowed Time; The Story of Britain Between the Wars*, Little, Brown, 2007.

Hattersley, Roy, *David Lloyd George; The Great Outsider*, Little, Brown, 2010.

Jeffrey, Keith (2008) *Field Marshal Sir Henry Wilson; A Political Soldier*, Oxford University Press, 2008.

Jenkins, Roy, *Churchill: A Biography*, Pan, 2012.

Kee, Robert, *Ireland: A History*, Weidenfeld & Nicolson, 1980.

Kinvig, Clifford, *Churchill's Crusade*, Hambledon Continuum, 2007.

Kleine, Joanne, *Invisible Men; The Daily Lives of Police Constables in Manchester, Birmingham and Liverpool*, Liverpool University Press, 2010.

Laybourn, Keith, *The General Strike Day by Day*, Sutton Publishing, 1996.

Madeira, Victor, *Britannia and the Bear; The Anglo-Russian Intelligence Wars, 1917-1929*, Boydell Press, 2014.

Moore, William, *The Thin Yellow Line*, Leo Cooper, 1974.

Moorehead, Alan, *The Russian Revolution*, Collins, 1958.

Neiberg, Michael S., *The World War I Reader*, New York University Press, 2006.

Neville, Peter, *Russia*, Windrush Press, 2002.

Priestly, J. B. (1970) *The Edwardians* London, William Heinemann, 1970.

Pugh, Martin, *We Danced All Night; A Social History of Britain Between the Wars*, Vintage, 2009.

Rayner, Ed, and Stapley, Ron, *Debunking History*, Sutton Publishing, 2002.

Reynolds, G. W. & Judge, Anthony, *The Night the Police went on Strike*, Weidenfeld and Nicolson, 1968.

Sheffield, Gary, *The Chief; Douglas Haig and the British Army*, Aurum Press, 2011.

Smith, Michael, *Station X; The Code Breakers of Bletchley Park*, Pan, 2004.

Snesarev, Andrei, *Afghanistan: Preparing for the Bolshevik Incursion into Afghanistan and India 1919-20*, Helion and Company, 2014.

Taylor, A. J. P., *The First World War*, George Rainbird, 1963.

Taylor A. J. P., *The Oxford History of England; English History 1914-1945*, Oxford University Press, 1965.

Toye, Richard, *Lloyd George & Churchill*, Macmillan, 2007.

Vallance, Edward, *A Radical History of Britain*, Little Brown, 2009.

Webb, Simon, *The Suffragette Bombers; Britain's Forgotten Terrorists*, Pen & Sword, 2014.

Webb, Simon, *Bombers, Rioters and Police Killers; Violent Crime and Disorder in Victorian Britain*, Pen & Sword, 2015.

White, Jerry, *Zeppelin Nights; London in the First World War*, The Bodley Head, 2014.

Index

INDEX